A Textbook of Generic Elective on Everyday Chemistry

Dr. Dnyaneshwar S. Wankhede
Associate Professor,
School of Chemical Sciences,
Swami Ramanand Teerth Marathwada University, Nanded (MS) INDIA.

Dr. Vikas D. Ragole
Assistant Professor
Late Ramesh Warpudkar Arts, Commerce and Science college,
Sonpeth, Dist. Parbhani (MS) INDIA.

NOTION PRESS

India. Singapore. Malaysia.

Preface

The authors take pleasure in presenting this book entitled, **"A Textbook of Generic Elective on Everyday Chemistry'** for B.Sc. First Year students. Swami Ramanand Teerth Marathwada University, Nanded has updated syllabus for 'Four year multiple degree programme with multiple entry and exit' for B.Sc. Degree as per NEP-2020 and implemented it effectively since 2024-25. The generic elective paper is a interdisciplinary course and will be opted by students from almost all faculties including Science, Arts and Commerce at B.Sc. First Year level. The aim of this course is to introduce students with multidisciplinary subjects and make them aware about knowledge other than their faculty specific courses.

The syllabus includes four modules viz. Soaps, detergents and cosmetics, Food additives and flavoring agents, Chemistry of plastics and Drugs chemistry of total 60 teaching hours. The syllabus is prepared with a view to introduce all students with chemistry involved in everyday life. The accessories, ingredients, articles or things used in our daily life, chemistry behind their synthesis or preparation, their applications and hazards regarding health or environment are inlcuded in these modules.

The book includes all the points mentioned in the syllabus with appropriate details. The aim is to help students in gaining knowledge about involvement of chemistry principles in daily life and motivate them to learn more about such things. The chemistry details are restricted to simple level so that other faculty students can cope with it, understand and face their examination. The english language used is simple and lucid so that every student can read and understand. The information provided in the book is also supported with the help of chemical structures and simple picture representations to help students.

As very few reading materials are available on these modules, help of various internet sources and blogs is taken and they are mentioned under 'References' section at the end of each module. In addition, question bank on each module is also provided at the end of the module to help students in their studies.

We are confident that the book will definitely help to the graduate students. It will create awareness and interest in them about chemistry principles applicable in daily life and motivate them. As such it will complement to fulfill the aim of curriculum designed by our university.

Dnyaneshwar Wankhede
Vikas Ragole
April 2025

Contents

CHAPTER- 1

Soaps, Detergents and cosmetics

Soaps: Introduction, fats and oils used in oaps, types of soaps, liquid soaps, synthesis of soaps, total fatty matter, cleaning action of soaps

Detergents: Introduction, classification, synthesis, additive in detergents, enzymatic detergents, cleaning action of detergents

Cosmetics: Introduction, toothpaste, shampoos, hair dyes, creams and lotions, lipstick, perfumes, shaving cream, after shave lotion, deodorants, bath oil, talcum powder.

Toxicity of detergents

Introduction

Everybody wants to look neat, clean and beautiful. Progress of science and technology has created awareness about self-image and cleanliness in human life. As such many commercial products has been developed to satisfy this urge. Soaps and detergents help us in cleaning our body, clothes and utensils while cosmetics help us in looking beautiful. In this chapter, we will learn about the chemistry behind all such products.

Soaps (साबण)

Soaps are sodium or potassium salts of long chain fatty acids. Soaps are surface active agents or surfactants which reduce surface tension between a liquid and another substance, thus causing foaming of solution and helping in emulsification of oils in water. This property helps soap solutions to remove dirt or soil particles adhered to the skin, clothes and other surfaces.

Fats and oils used in soaps (साबणांमध्ये वापरले जाणारे चरबी आणि तेले)

Generally, fats and oils from vegetables and animals are used in soap making process. Table 1 listed the various fats and oils used and their properties in soap making process.

Table 1. Fats & Oils used in soap making

Fatty acid	Type	Oil	Property
Lauric acid $(C_{12}H_{24}O_2)$	Saturated	Coconut oil, Palm kernel oil, babassu oil	Hardening, cleansing, gives big & fluffy lather
Myristic acid $[C_{14}H_{28}O_2]$	Saturated	Murumuru butter, tucuma seed butter, monoi de Tahiti oil, cohune oil	Hardening, cleansing, gives fluffy lather
Palmitic acid $[C_{16}H_{32}O_2]$	Saturated	Coconut butter, palm oil, grapeseed oil,	Hardening, gives creamy lather
Stearic acid $[C_{18}H_{36}O_2]$	Saturated	Shea butter, soybean oil, kokum oil, illipe butter, sal fat, mango butter	Hardening, gives stable lather
Oleic acid $[C_{18}H_{34}O_2]$	Unsaturated	Olive oil, sunflower oil, safflower oil, canola oils, sweet almond oil, grapeseed oil	Conditioning, moisturising, gives slippery lather
Linoleic acid $[C_{18}H_{32}O_2]$	Unsaturated	Hemp oil, Sweet almond oil	Conditioning, moisturising, gives silky lather
Linolenic acid $[C_{18}H_{30}O_2]$	Unsaturated	Sunflower oil, hemp oil, olive oil, grapeseed oil, pomegranate seed oil, flax oil	Conditioning, moisturising, gives silky lather
Ricin oleic acid $[C_{18}H_{34}O_3]$	Unsaturated	Castor oil	Conditioning, moisturising, gives slippery lather

Types of soaps (साबणांचे प्रकार)

A variety of soaps viz. washing soaps, toilet soaps, medicated soaps, beauty soaps, industrial soaps etc. are available in the market today. The simple classification, based on applications, includes the following:

1. Washing soaps (धुण्याचे साबण)

Washing soaps are prepared by reacting oils and fats with sodium hydroxide. The various ingredients are alkali, fillers like Na_2CO_3, silicate, clays, optical whiteners etc. The composition in general is 20% soap, 40% soda ash (Na_2CO_3) and 40% water as water of crystallization. These soaps are used for washing clothes, cleaning utensils, floors etc.

2. Toilet soaps (टॉयलेट साबण)

Toilet soaps are used for personal care such as washing of hands, face or for bathing. They are obtained using sodium hydroxide and vegetable or animal fats. The other components include perfume, colour and preservatives to stabilize it. Examples, common daily soaps such as Lux,

3. Medicated soaps (औषधी साबण)

The soaps used for preventing or treating skin infections, acne etc. are called as medicated soaps. These are also effective in removing excess oil, dirt and impurities from the skin. These soaps include special antiseptic or similar ingredients and can kill bacteria on the skin surfaces.

4. Industrial soaps (औद्योगिक साबण)

These soaps are useful for cleaning industrial machinery. These are also applicable as wetting agents in textile industry. For example, soaps including calcium and aluminium soaps are used as water repellents in the manufacture of waterproof textiles and walls, zinc and magnesium stearate soap is used in face powders, the soaps used for sizing (which act as protective filler or glaze for paper) are made from oils like coconut, castor, olive and ground nut oils.

Liquid soaps (द्रव साबण)

Soaps available in liquid form are called as liquid soaps. These are potassium salt of fatty acids and generally used for washing of hands or body. Examples include Dettol hand wash, Dettol body wash, Lux body wash, Dove body wash, Fiama body wash etc.

Liquid soaps has gained importance in daily life due to various reasons as listed below:

1. Liquid soaps are easy to use.

2. Liquid soaps contain preservatives which prevent the growth of bacteria, Mold, and mildew.

3. Liquid soaps are available in a wide variety of formulations, scents, and colours, thus providing options for users to choose as per their preferences.

4. Liquid soaps contain additional cleansing agents and moisturizers which give more thorough cleaning experience.

5. Liquid soaps are easy to transport and use in various set ups such as travel, gyms, or workplaces.

6. Liquid soaps can be efficiently dispensed and used, leading to less waste.

Due to all these properties, liquid soaps are popular and widely used.

Synthesis of soaps (साबणांचे संश्लेषण)

Soap is synthesized using saponification process. The word 'sapo' is a Latin word which means soap. In chemistry, the reaction of an ester with water and a base such as NaOH or KOH to produce alcohol and the sodium or potassium salt of an acid is called saponification.

In this process, fats and oils from vegetable and animal sources are reacted with a liquid alkali to produce soap and water (neat soap) plus glycerine. (Reaction)

$$\begin{array}{ccccc}
CH_2-O-\overset{O}{\overset{\|}{C}}-R & & & & Na^+\ ^-O-\overset{O}{\overset{\|}{C}}-R \\
| & & & & \\
CH-O-\overset{O}{\overset{\|}{C}}-R' & +\ 3\ NaOH & \rightarrow & CH-OH & +\ Na^+\ ^-O-\overset{O}{\overset{\|}{C}}-R' \\
| & & & | & \\
CH_2-O-\overset{O}{\overset{\|}{C}}-R'' & & & CH_2OH & Na^+\ ^-O-\overset{O}{\overset{\|}{C}}-R'' \\
\text{Fat} & \text{alkali} & & \text{glycerol} & \text{soap}
\end{array}$$

Total Fatty Matter (TFM)

Total fatty matter or TFM is a parameter used to represent the fatty matter present in soaps. The fatty matters come from the vegetable oils and fatty acids like stearic acid, palmitic acid, sodium oleate and oleic acid or triglycerides present in soaps. When mineral acids such as hydrochloric acid is added to soap, the fatty matter gets separated. The amount of this fatty matter separated is given by TFM.

The fatty matter available in soaps help to clean our body without drying it and are responsible for the moisturizing effect of a soap. Thus, TFM is an important parameter to decide quality of our soap. The higher the TFM percentage the less harmful it is for our skin.

Role of total fatty matter (TFM) in soap:

The role of TFM content in soap can be explained based on following points:

1. Cleansing effect: (साफ करणारे प्रभाव)

The higher TFM content in soaps creates more lather and form lathers more and form micelles which traps the dirt and removes it. Thus, have more cleansing effect.

2. Skincare benefits: (त्वचेची काळजी घेण्याचे फायदे)

The higher TFM content in soaps provides better moisturizing effects, thus soaps are less harsh on skin. This reduces the dryness and irritation of skin and helps it to remain soft and hydrated.

3. Longevity: (दीर्घायुष्य)

The higher TFM content facilitate soaps to last longer. Thus, soaps do not dissolve quickly and are cost-effective.

4. Fragrance and Texture: (सुगंध आणि बनावट)

The high TFM content provide soaps long-lasting fragrance quality and smoother and luxurious texture. This helps in giving a better bathing experience.

In short, total fatty matters or TFM is an indicator which tells us how good or bad a soap is for our skin.

Cleaning action of soaps (साबणांची स्वच्छता क्रिया)

Soaps are amphiphilic. Amphiphilic molecules have both hydrophilic (water loving) and hydrophobic (water hating) properties. Soaps are sodium or potassium salts of long chain fatty acids and can be represented to have head and tail structure (fig).

The ($-Coo-Na^+$) group represents the polar head and the long chain part [$(CH_2)_n$] represents the non-polar tail in soaps. The head is hydrophilic (water loving), while the tail is hydrophobic (water hating) in nature. Due to both these groups, viz. hydrophilic and hydrophobic, soaps do not dissolve in water. In fact, on vigorous shaking, they can disperse in water and form micelles.

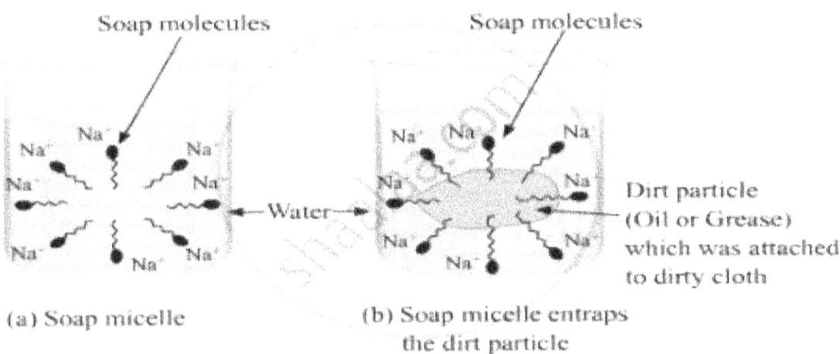

The polar hydrophobic heads of micelles interact with water molecules at the surface and non-polar hydrophobic tails remain away from water. This micelles formation gives soaps its cleansing property. The dirt or soil particles are attached to the skin, cloth and other surfaces with the help of some greasy materials like oil, cooking fats, sweet etc. Since oils are not miscible with water, washing with water alone will not help. The micelles reduce the surface tension of water and as a result, the wetting ability of water increases. Due to this, soap molecules wet the dirt and soil particles and remove them from the surface.

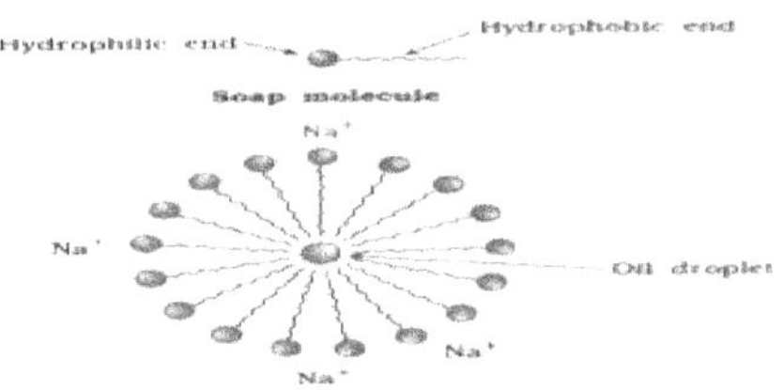

Fig. cleansing action of soaps

Detergents (डिटर्जंट्स)

The term detergent is used in a general sense to refer any surfactant i.e. surface active (chemical) agent which can remove dirt from the surface. Soap was the first known detergent. Surfactants clean the surface by reducing surface tension at the boundary between two phases. So, soap, detergents, emulsifiers, wetting agents and penetrants are all surfactants, because they modify the properties.

In modern days, detergent generally refers to synthetic detergent or syndet. A surfactant or a mixture of surfactants with cleansing properties in dilute solutions is called as detergent. Unlike soaps, detergents are more soluble in hard water and hence more effective. In our daily use, the term 'detergent' refers to, the one used for laundry or dish wash purposes. Detergents are also amphiphilic i.e. containing both hydrophilic and hydrophobic parts and hence their cleansing action is also like soaps.

Classification of detergents (डिटर्जंट्सचे वर्गीकरण)

Detergents or synthetic detergents are broadly classified into three groups, viz. anionic, cationic and non-ionic detergents based on the electrical charge of the surfactants.

1. Anionic detergents

These mainly includes alkylbenzenesulfonates (ABS). In these detergents, the alkylbenzene portion is lipophilic (i.e. lipids loving or hydrophobic or water hating) and the sulfonate portion is hydrophilic (water loving). These are very popular and average annual production is around 6 billion kilograms.

2. Cationic detergents

These are like the anionic ones but include quaternary ammonium group instead of anionic sulfonate group, hence called as cationic detergents. The ammonium sulfate center is positively charged.

3. Non-ionic and Zwitter ionic detergents

These are based on polyoxyethylene or a glycoside and are characterized by uncharged, hydrophilic headgroups. Common examples include,

Polyoxyethylene based: Tween, Triton, and the Brij series.

Glycoside bases: octylthioglucoside, maltosides.

Zwitterionic detergents include CHAPS i.e. 3-[(3-cholamidopropyl) dimethylammonio]-1-propanesulfonate in their structure. These possess a net zero charge arising from the presence of equal numbers of unipositive (+1) and uninegative (-1) groups.

Synthesis of detergents

Synthetic detergents viz. anionic and non-ionic detergents are synthesized through following processes:

1. Anionic detergents

Fats are ester of fatty acids or a mixture of such compounds, commonly found in living beings or in food. Fats are solid at room temperature. Fats are either saturated or unsaturated. The unsaturated fats that are liquid at room temperature are called as oils. Unsaturated fats may be of monosaturated or polysaturated types. The hydrocarbons from fats and oils or from petroleum products are extracted. These extracted hydrocarbons are then undergoing chemical reaction to produce acids. These acids are like fatty acids. In next step, alkali liquid is used to produce an anionic detergent.

2. Non-ionic surfactants

In this case, the hydrocarbons from fats and oils or from petroleum products are extracted. These extracted hydrocarbons are converted to alcohol using chemical reaction and then are reacted with ethylene oxide. After this, sulphur containing acids are reacted with them to produce non-ionic detergents.

Additives in detergents

Detergent is a mixture of different chemicals. Detergents are composed of many ingredients including builders, surfactants, bleach, enzymes, soil anti-deposition agents, foam regulators, corrosion inhibitors, optical brighteners, dye transfer inhibitors, fragrances, dyes, fillers and formulation aids etc. The various ingredients are discussed in brief as follows:

1. Builders: Hard water contains various metallic ions including calcium, magnesium, iron, copper and manganese. These metal ions react with surfactant anions to form insoluble compounds or precipitates, difficult to be removed, which gets deposited on fabrics and washing machines.   Builders also called as chelating or sequestering agents, are water softeners which are used for water softening. The above-mentioned hard water ions are removed by builders using precipitation, chelation or ion exchange processes. In addition, they also remove soil dispersion. Examples include sodium carbonate (washing soda) and sodium silicate (waterglass), sodium phosphates, polyphosphates (sodium hexametaphosphate).

2. Surfactants: These are mostly responsible for the cleaning action of detergents. Anionic and non-ionic surfactants are mostly used. Cationic surfactants have poor cleaning efficiency and are used for certain special cases such as fabric softeners, antistatic agents, and biocides. Zwitterionic surfactants are mainly used to reduce the cost factor. A combination of various surfactants to balance their performance and to have better effect is used.

3. Bleaches: The bleaches used mainly targets oxidisable organic stains, for example, chlorophyll, anthocyanin dyes, tannins, humic acids, and carotenoid pigments etc. which are from vegetable origin mainly. Common examples include stable hydrogen peroxide adducts viz. sodium perborate and sodium percarbonate. These are stable in solid state, but release hydrogen peroxide on reaction with water. As hydrogen peroxide is inactive below $60^{\circ}C$, bleach activators such as tetraacetylethylenediamine (TAED), which react with hydrogen peroxide to produce peracetic acid, which is more effective bleaching agent at low temperatures is used these days.

4. Enzymes: Otto Rohm, in 1913, used a pancreatic extract obtained from slaughtered animals in detergents. The extract was unstable against alkali and bleach. This was first incidence when enzymes were used as additives in detergents. Today with the advent of science and technology, the application of enzymes as additive in detergents is common.

Enzymes in detergents are useful for degradation of the stubborn stains composed of proteins (milk, cocoa blood, egg yolk, grass), fats (chocolate, fats, oils), starch (flour and potato stains) and cellulose (damaged cotton fibrils, vegetable and fruit stains). A different type of enzyme is to be used for each type of different stain. The common enzymes include proteases (savinase) for proteins, lipases for greases, α-amylases for carbohydrates and cellulases for cellulose.

5. Corrosion Inhibitors (गंज प्रतिबंधक) : These are used to protect the washing equipment from damage.

6. Dye Transfer Inhibitors: These are used to prevent dye from one article to colour another article.

7. Anti-redeposition agents: These are used to prevent fine soil particles from reattaching to the product after being cleaned.

8. Perfumes: These are used to remove bad smell and to add specific aroma to the fabric after cleaning. Common examples of perfume used are terpene alcohols (citronellol, geraniol, linallol, nerol) and their esters (linalyl acetate), aromatic aldehydes (helional, hexyl cinnamaldehyde, lilial) and synthetic musks (galaxolide) etc.

9. Optical brighteners: These are used to add brightness and whiteness to white fabrics. Examples include fluorescent dyes.

10. Foam control agent: These are used to control foaming in a detergent. Example, silicones.

Enzymatic detergents

Enzymatic detergents are biological compounds which are used to remove stains due to organic waste. They include a combination of various enzymes capable of removing stains from specific category. They may be of natural origin or synthetic. They act as catalysts for the chemical reaction useful for breaking down of dirt and tough stains during washing, which helps the detergents to clean these stains. These are also known as biological detergents.

Enzymatic detergents work in presence of moisture, need to be activated before use to have cleaning effect and take time to work i.e. 15 minutes to 8 hours based on type and severity of stains. They should not be used on fabrics like rayon or silk or on surfaces which cannot get wet.

Enzymes used in enzymatic detergents

The various types of enzymes commonly used for this purpose are listed below:

1. Protease: These enzymes are useful for removing protein stains such as egg and milk, mud or grass, meat juices, blood and other body fluid.

2. α-Amylase: These enzymes are useful for removing starch stains such as those left by gravy, cereal or pasta.

3. Pectate Lyase: These enzymes are useful for removing pectin stains which are left by fruits and vegetables.

4. Lipase: These enzymes are useful for removing stains on food stains such as butter and oils and other oils-based stains for example of lipstick and certain cosmetics. In shorts, these enzymes mainly target fats or lipids.

5. Mannanase: These enzymes useful for removing stains of sugars used as stabilizer food items viz. ketchup and ice creams, and personal care products like deodorants.

Cleansing action of detergents

Detergents or synthetic detergents, like soaps, have a long non-polar hydrocarbon chain and a highly polar group at the end. Hard water contains various metal ions such as Ca (II), Mg (II) and Fe (III) which form insoluble salts or precipitates with soaps. Detergents do not form insoluble salts with these ions. Thus, soaps can be used for soft water and face problems in hard water, whereas detergents can be used in both soft and hard water and have better cleansing power in comparison to ordinary soaps.

The cleansing action of detergents can be explained like those soaps. The detergents when dissolved in water, get dissociated into cations and anions. The anion part, i.e. long chain of hydrocarbon is hydrophobic (insoluble in water or water hating) in nature, is directed towards centre. The head part is hydrophilic (water loving) is on the surface. Thus, giving rise to micelles. This formation of micelles is responsible for cleansing action of detergents.

The micelles and grease or dirt in cloth, both are polar, gets attracted and micelles are absorbed in grease or dirt. Rubbing by hands of clothes or mechanical stirring in washing machines break the grease of dirt particles into smaller particles and form emulsion with water. As a result, the dirt or grease particles are removed away with washing water and clothes are cleaned.

Cosmetics (सौंदर्य प्रसाधने)

Introduction

Cosmetic are preparations used for beautifying or altering the appearance of human body. Since for ancient times, human being is interested in improving their looks or taking self-care of the body. In this regard, the natural or chemical preparations used for beautifying, preserving, or altering the appearance or for cleansing, colouring, conditioning, or protecting the skin, hair, nails, lips, eyes or teeth are called as cosmetics.

Evidence suggested the use of cosmetics in ancient Egypt and Rome since many years back. Applications of Kohl to darken the eyelashes, eyebrows and to outline the eyelids were known and was a preparation based on lampblack or antimony. Similarly, Rogue and various white powders applicable to redden the cheeks and to improve fairness of complexion were also in use. In addition, various bath oils, abrasives useful as dentifrices and perfumes were also known. All these can be called as cosmetics. In short, any substance used to clean, improve or change the complexion, skin, hair, nails or teeth are cosmetics.

Toothpaste (टूथपेस्ट)

A paste of gel dentifrice used for cleaning of teeth to keep them healthy and good looking is called as toothpaste. Toothpaste generally protects the enamel of teeth and maintains oral hygiene. Instead of using alone or with bare hands, it is better to use it with a toothbrush.

Food products that we eat get stuck in our teeth and gums and create plaque. The abrasives used as ingredient in toothpaste helps in removing these plaque and food from the teeth. The most common and active ingredient in toothpaste is fluoride which helps to prevent tooth decay (dental caries) and gum diseases.

The three main ingredients in toothpastes are abrasives, fluoride, and detergent.

1. Abrasives (अपघर्षक)

Abrasives are insoluble particles used to remove plaque from teeth, thus minimize the risk of gum disease. They constitute 8-20% part of a typical toothpaste. Common examples include aluminium hydroxide [$Al(OH)_3$], calcium carbonate ($CaCO_3$), magnesium carbonate ($MgCO_3$), sodium bicarbonate (Na_2CO_3), various calcium hydrogen phosphates, various silicas and zeolites, and hydroxyapatite [$Ca_5(PO_4)_3OH$].

2. Fluoride

One of the important ingredients of toothpaste is fluoride. It is a mineral which helps in preventing tooth decay. The amount of fluoride essential for a human being is dependent on person's age and other factor. Generally considered as safe, the excess amount of fluoride can lead to fluorosis. In fluorosis, one can experience brown stains on teeth along with pain and stiffness of teeth.

3. Detergents

Detergents are also essential ingredients of toothpaste. As we know, detergents are surfactants i.e. surface-active agents. They help to remove oil, blood, dust and other types of grime that accumulates on teeth. These contaminants can cause mouth infections which can be problematic. Detergents in toothpaste help to reduce this risk. Common examples include, sodium lauryl sulphate (SDS), cocamidopropyl betain, sodium methyl cocoyl taurate (adinol) etc.

Other ingredients present in toothpaste include antibacterial agents (Triclosan, Zinc chloride), flavouring agents (peppermint, spearmint, wintergreen), remineralizers (hydroxyapatite nanoparticles and calcium phosphate) etc.

Shampoos

Shampoos are used to keep hair and scalp clean by removing dirt, oil, and other residues. In addition, shampoo can help to condition and beautify the hairs. These are typically viscous coloured liquids. They are applied to wet hairs, massaged in and then rinsed with clean water. Shampoo contains surfactants, viz. sodium lauryl sulfate or sodium laureth sulfate, as cleaning agent and sulfate for creating a lather to remove oil from the hair.

Ingredients in a shampoo

The various ingredients in shampoos can be listed as below.

1. Carrying agents.

Generally, water is the carrying agent, but many shampoos also contain alcohols such as ethanol, propanol, isopropanol etc. Fatty alcohols such as cetyl alcohol, lauryl alcohol, cetearyl alcohol and stearyl alcohol are useful as they all are known to lock in moisture.

2. Thickeners

Thickeners are used to increase the flow of the shampoo. Common examples include stearic acid, gelatin, xanthum gum, carnauba wax, stearyl alcohol, cetyl alcohol etc.

3. Surfactants

Surfactants make shampoos effective cleaners. They are drying agents useful for removing oil from hair. Common examples include ammonium lauryl sulfate, sodium laureth sulfate, ammonium laureth sulfate, sodium trideceth sulfate.

4. Preservatives (संरक्षक)

These are used to stop Mold, a health hazard, from growing in shampoos. Common examples include sodium benzoate and potassium sorbate.

Parabens are also used as preservatives. Recently the research indicated the use of parabens can lead to breast cancer. Examples include methylparaben, propylparaben, isopropylparaben, ethylparaben, isobutylparaben, butylparaben etc.

5. Emolients (उत्तेजित करणारा)

These help our hair follicles to keep some moisture, stop them from becoming brittle, lubricate the strands of our hair and stop damage. Overall, emollients make our hair looks shinier and lively. Common examples include aloe vera, vegetable and minerals oils and silicone (dimethicone).

Adverse effects of shampoos

The long-term use of shampoo can lead to adverse effects. The various ingredients causing serious health concerns on long term use are listed below.

1. Sulphates: Make hairs dry and increase skin sensitivity.

2. Parabens: Increase risk of skin cancer.

3. Phthalates: Cause hormonal disruptions and are also dangerous to the environment.

4. Formaldehyde: Cause cancer.

5. Alcohol: Makes hair dry and brittle.

6. Retinyl palmitate: Cause itching, scaling and peeling.

7. Toluene: Can hamper immune system and cause congenital problems.

Hair dyes

The cosmetic products used to change the colour of hair are called as hair dyes or hair colours. These are mainly used to colour grey hairs or to change the natural colour of hair. We should know that the two types of melanin protein, Eumelanin and Phaeomelanin, present in hair are responsible for hair colour and absence of these pigments results in white or grey hair.

Keratin, a hard and fibrous protein insoluble in water, is the main component of hair. It constitutes almost 95% of human hair and is useful for ensuring protection of human hair. The hair shaft is comprised of three layers viz. Medulla, Cortex and Cuticle. The Cortex and Medulla are known to hold hair pigments and are responsible for hair colour.

Common hair dye contains two main chemical ingredients viz. hydrogen peroxide (H_2O_2) and ammonia (NH_3). Hydrogen peroxide (30% volume or lower) oxidizes the natural melanin pigments in hair and make them colourless, which helps new permanent colour to form bonds with hair cortex. Ammonia helps the dye molecules to induce more permanent colouring by after passing into hairs.

Side effects of hair dyes

Modern hair dyes contain various chemicals such as p-phenylenediamine, ethanolamine, ammonia, hydrogen peroxide, resorcinol, parabens, lead (II) acetate, sodium laurate sulphate, titanium oxide and phthalates etc. These various ingredients in hair dyes can cause harmful health effects. The common health effects can be listed as below:

1. Ammonia can trigger asthma attacks, toluene is a neurotoxin that may be linked to congenital abnormalities, pregnancy loss, and allergic reactions or dermatitis etc.

2. In some cases, hair dye can damage hair strands, causing hair to break off, while in some cases hair can become dull, brittle and dead.

3. The various chemicals can disrupt the endocrine system and can cause cancer, especially women frequently using hair dyes have a high risk of breast cancer.

4. In case, the hair dyes are swallowed or absorbed into the blood through the skin hair poisoning may occur. If get into the eyes, hair dyes can cause conjunctivitis.

Creams and lotions

Creams and lotions form major portion of the cosmetics in modern world. They are semi-solid emulsions of oil-water and used to improve the skin health and make it smoother and softer. They provide skin a moisturized appearance by keeping it hydrated. The common skin issues such as dryness and oiliness can be overcome by application of creams and lotions. The application method is simple, and one can simply apply creams and lotions on to skin by massaging with our hands.

Body creams and body lotions differ in composition and consistency. The main differences between body creams and body lotions can be listed as below:

1. Body creams have less water content; body lotions have more water content.

2. Body creams have more oil content; body lotions have less oil content.

3. Body creams are heavier in consistency compared to body lotions.

4. Body creams last longer on the body as compared to body lotions.

5. Body creams keeps our skin hydrated more compared to body lotions.

6. Body creams are more suitable for winter, while body lotions are better for summer.

Lipstick

Lipstick is a cosmetic product applied to lips to colour and texture them. It is often made using wax and oil. It is used to shield the lips from external elements such as wind, cold and pollution. It nourishes our lips, locks moisture and keeps them hydrated. Lipsticks typically contains three main ingredients including wax, oil, and colour pigment.

1. Wax: Wax is responsible for giving lipstick shape and grip, creating gloss, and making it smooth. Common examples include beeswax, carnauba wax, candelia wax and tallow wax etc.

2. Oils: Oils in lipstick help to moisturize, soften and dissolve colourants and other solvents in the lipsticks. Common examples include castor oil, grapeseed oil, almond oil, palm oil, olive oil, cocoa butter, jojoba, lanolin etc.

3. Colour pigments or colourants: They help to colour the lips. They are of two types of inorganic and organic colourants. Common examples of inorganic colourants include iron oxide, titanium dioxide, zinc oxide, pearl powder. They are insoluble and appropriate preparation techniques are required to disperse them evenly on the lips. Common examples of organic colourants include beetroot red, anthocyanins, lactoflavin etc. They are soluble and easily dispersed. The disadvantage is that they can cause colour smearing and often combined.

In addition, some preservatives, antioxidants and fragrances are also added to the lipsticks. The preservatives and antioxidants maintain longevity of the lipstick, while fragrances mask the scent of chemicals in oils, waxes and colourants in lipsticks.

Perfumes

The combination of organic compounds used to produce pleasant and desirable smell or odour is called as perfume or fragrance. A perfume is obtained from fragrant essential oils derived from plants and spices or synthetic aromatic compounds. The regular use of perfumes is intended to increase self-appeal and self-confidence of an individual. Perfumes also known to improve one's mood reducing anxiety and stress.

Adverse effects of perfume

The frequent use of perfume can cause many adverse effects.

1. The various chemicals in perfumes are directly absorbed on skin on frequent application which can cause allergic dermatitis.

2. In addition, headache, migraine, dizziness, congestion, rashes, eye, nose and throat irritation, nausea, asthma flares etc. can result due frequent perfume use.

3. Body perfumes when used for longer period may lead to a range of health problems including allergies, lung disease, organ damage and even cancer.

Shaving cream

Shaving creams and soaps are cosmetics used for shaving preparation to wet and soften the beard by providing lubrication. Shaving creams produce rich foam which helps hold the facial hair erect for cutting. Shaving creams are generally applied using shaving brush, although brushless shaving creams are also an option in modern days. Shaving creams and soaps are available in many forms including bars, creams, in tubes or aerosols. They contain 20-30% soap [sodium or potassium steareate or triethanolamine (TEA)], 10% glycerine, emollients, emulsifiers, and foaming agents.

Different types of shaving creams include aerosol shaving cream (shaving foam), lather less shaving cream (brushless shaving cream and non-aerosol shaving cream), and lather shaving cream or lathering shaving cream.

Aftershave lotion

Aftershave lotions are cosmetic products used to make skin soft and freshen it after shaving. It is generally used by men. These are available in variety of forms such as liquid, lotion, gel or even a paste.

Typical aftershave products are alcohol-based, in which alcohol close the skin pores and prevent irritation caused due to razor use. Commonly ethyl alcohol or isopropyl alcohol is used. These work as antibacterial agents and kill bacteria or toxins on face skin after shave. As ethanol is toxic and can lead to excessive oral ingestion, alcohol-free aftershave products are also launched in the market.

Application of aftershave is a simple process and includes rinsing the face with cold water, drying it with clean towel and apply right amount of aftershave product with hands on face skin.

Deodorants

Deodorants are cosmetics useful to get relief from sweating and bad body odour. These are normally applied topically in armpits and reduce the production of sweat. In this way, they are known to affect the body function and hence considered as over the counter drug by FDA.

We should know that the sweat is clear, salty liquid which is odourless. It is mostly water, with small amounts of salt and other substances. The production of sweat is an important body process useful for regulating body temperature. The bad smell or body odour is resultant mixture of sweat with bacteria and yeast on our skin and most often occurs in body areas such as armpits, groin, feet, genitals, belly button, anus and behind the ears. Maintaining good hygiene by regular washing, changing sweaty clothing as early as possible and application of cosmetics such as antiperspirants and deodorants can reduce the body odour.

Deodorants are available in variety of forms such as sticks, roll-ons, gels/creams and aerosols etc. Deodorants should be able to deliver effective and uniform delivery of product in the underarm area, stable for reasonable length of time, aesthetically appealing and should be safe to body as well as clothing.

Side effects of deodorants

Although deodorants are very safe, still some side effects are possible. As per the American Cancer Society (ACS) these products can cause nonspecific irritant reactions and sensitizations leading to allergic contact dermatitis (ACD) due to chemicals viz. fragrance, propylene glycol and vitamin E or tocopherol, included in deodorants.

Bath oil

The scented oils added to water during bath are called as bath oils. They are special cleansing products used for body wash. They are generally made from natural ingredients helpful for moisturizing and making skin soft.

Bathing with oil, known as Abhyanga Snana, is part of our tradition since ancient times. Taking oil bath is an effective way to relax after a long and exhausting day. It helps in great way to ease muscle aches and pains. It includes applying simple cleansing oil to the skin which helps in nourishing, moisturizing and hydrating it. The process helps in detoxification, rejuvenation and relaxation of the body.

Examples of various oils used include eucalyptus oil, lavender oil, lemon oil, sesame oil, coconut oil etc.

Talcum powder

Talcum powder, a widely used cosmetic product, is a powder made from talc. It is used for keeping skin dry by absorbing moisture. Talc is a mineral, called as hydrated magnesium silicate, composed of magnesium, silicon and oxygen. Talc is usually green, white, gray, brown or colourless. It is softest mineral.

Talc is crushed, dried and milled into a fine, soft and white powder called as talcum powder. Talcum powder can absorb oils, moisture, odour, reduce friction and also make the products feel silky. Hence it is used in a variety of cosmetic products such as in baby powder, adult body and face powders, makeup, deodorants, ceramics and paints.

Is Talc safe?

Some talc may contain asbestos as ingredient. Asbestos is known carcinogen i.e. cancer-causing agent and regular use can lead to endometrial and ovarian cancer. Also, talc exposure can lead to tumour formation in lungs, stomach and heart. Such talcum powders should be avoided. Some manufacturers provide asbestos-free talcum powders which are useful, although long term use should be avoided.

Question Bank

1. What are soaps? What are ingredients in soaps?

2. Enlist various fats and oils used in soap making.

3. Give various types of soaps.

4. What is mean by liquid soaps?

5. What is mean by total fatty matter (TFM)? What is its significance?

6. How is soap prepared? Explain cleansing action of soaps.

7. Define detergents. Give types of detergents.

8. Discuss variou additives in detergents.

9. What is mean by enzymatic detergents? Enlist various application of enzymatic detergents.

10. Which enzymes are used in enzymatic detergents?

11. Explain toxicity of detergents.

12. What are cosmetics? Enlist various cosmetics we use in our daily life.

13. What is toothpaste? What are main ingredients in toothpaste?

14. What is shampoo? Discuss various ingredients in shampoo.

15. Give adverse effects of shampoo.

16. What are hair dyes? Give classification of hair dyes.

17. Discuss side effects of hair dyes.

18. What is lipstick? What are main ingredients in lipstick?

19. Define perfumes. Give classification of perfumes.

20. Explain chemical structure of perfumes.

21. How is perfume manufactured?

22. What is shaving cream? Explain total fatty sustance (TFS).

23. What are aftershave cosmetics? Enlist various ingredients in aftershave cosmetics.

24. What are deodorants? Explain various ingredients present in deodorants.

25. What are bath oils? What are benefits of using bath oils?

26. What is talcum powder? Is it safe?

References

1. https://en.wikipedia.org

2. https://www.cosmebio.org

3. https://byjus.com

4. https://www.foodcircle.com

5. https://chem.libretexts.org

6. https://www.vedantu.com

7. https://consumeraffairs.nic.in

8. https://unacademy.com

9. https://britannica.com

10. https://thoughtco.com

11. https://www.embibe.com

12. https://www.sigmaaldrich.com

13. https://www.ecos.com

14. https://www.webmd.com

15. https://www.johnsons-me.com

16. https://www.vinmec.com

17. https://dermnetnz.org

18. https://www.cosmeticsinfo.org

CHAPTER- 2

Food additives and flavouring agents

Syllabus: *Introduction, food colours, flavouring agents, emulsifying agents, preservative, leavening agents, test enhancers, antioxidants.*

Government regulations.

Soft drinks, its ingredients and health effects.

Food adulteration, food laws and standards.

Prevention of food adulteration (PFA) Act 1954

Essentials commodities act 1955

Food and safety and standards act 2006

Introduction

Food colours (खाद्य रंग)

The substances or additives added to food products, and which are responsible for their colours are called as food colours or food colouring agents. It is well known that food properties viz. freshness, safety, nutritional value, taste, and texture etc. play an important role in determining its' quality by increasing acceptability and making it more fascinating for consumers. Food colours are responsible for not only changing colour, but also in maintaining or improving nutritional value, taste, texture and appearance of food products. They are used in different forms viz. liquids, liquid gel dye, powders, gels and pastes etc.

Classification of food colours (खाद्य रंगांचे वर्गीकरण)

Food colours are generally classified into two types viz. natural or synthetic food colours.

a. Natural food colours

Natural food colours are extracted from various naturally occurring sources including seeds, flowers, vegetables, insects, algae and minerals etc. Their preparation methods are simple with minimum chemical reactions. In addition, they are bio disposable which increases their demand in the food industry. For example, anthocyanins, betacyanin's, carotenoids and phenolic compounds are examples of natural food colours.

The use of natural food colours has certain limitations such as lack of consistent colour intensities, instability to light and heat exposure, variability of supply, reactivity with other food components, and addition of secondary flavours and odours. Also, many of them are insoluble in water and need to be used in presence of an emulsifier.

b. Synthetic food colours

Synthetic food colours are man-made and obtained from minerals, petrochemicals, petroleum and coal tar sources. They are water-soluble and are available commercially as powders, pastes, granules, or solutions. Their stability is affected by light, heat, pH, and reducing agents.

They are available in different shades and aid bright and tempting colours to the food products. In addition, they are cheap and easily available in large quantities compared to natural food colours. This has increased their demand in food industry.

But their use in large amounts cause pollution issues by disturbing ecological balance and their toxic nature can lead to harmful diseases such as behavioural problems, depression, food allergies, headaches and migraines, and brain tumours etc. Figure 1 given below represents chemical structures of few food colours.

Anthrocyanin structure   Betacyanin structure

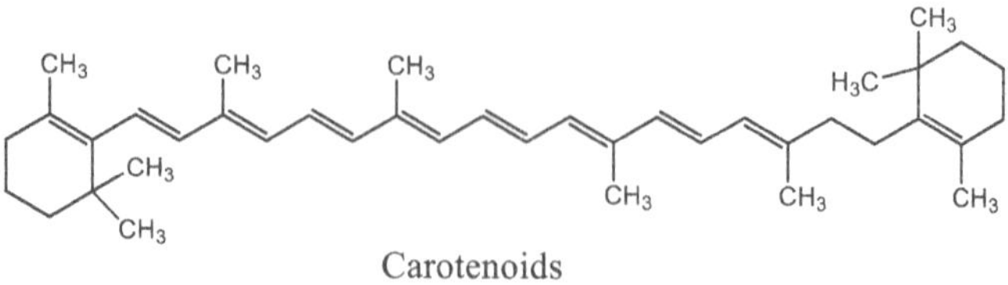

Carotenoids

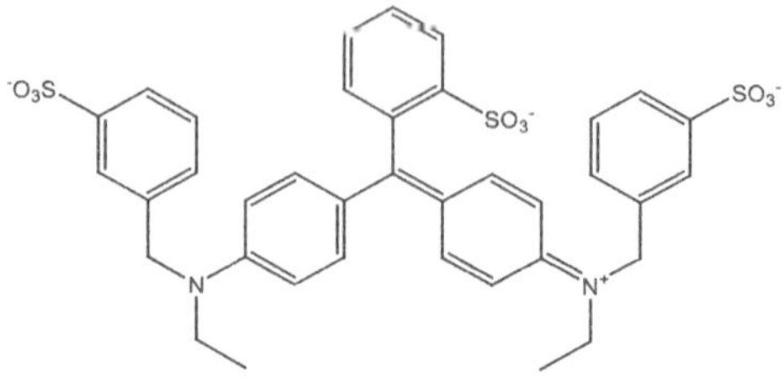

Brilliant Blue FCF

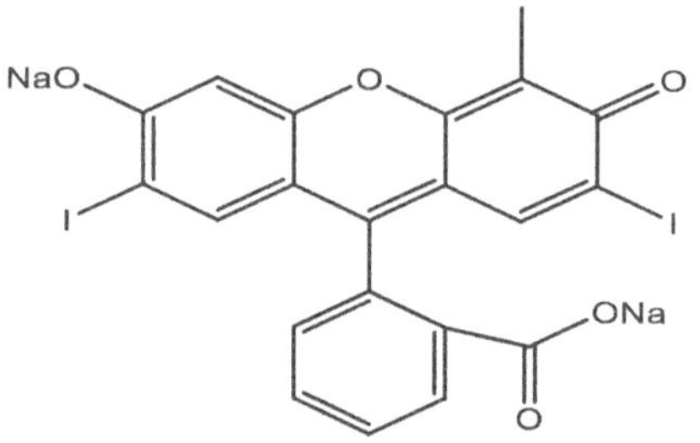

Erythrosine

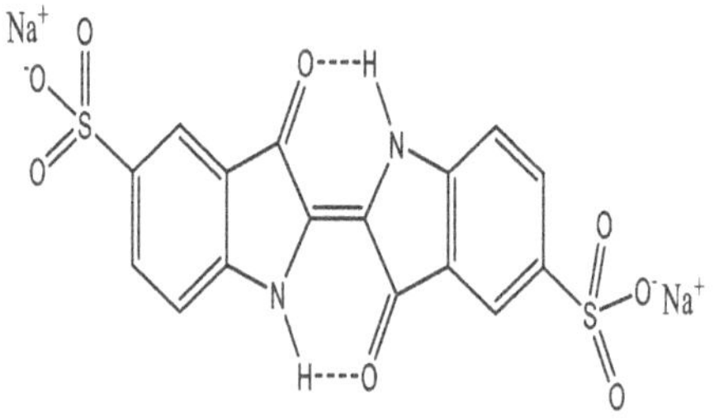

Indigocarmine

Figure 1. Chemical structures of Food colours

Few important natural and synthetic food colours along with their colours and food products in which they are used are listed in Table 1.

Table 1. Food colours, their colours and food products

Natural food colours (colour)	Food products	Synthetic food colours (colour)	Food products
Anthocyanins (Blue-reddish shades)	Soft drinks, alcoholic drinks, pickles	Allura red AC (Red)	Gelatine, puddings, dairy products, confections, beverages
Annatto (Orange shades)	Dairy and fat products and desserts	Brilliant blue FCF (Blue)	Beverages, confections, icings, syrups, dairy products
Beta-carotene (Yellow-orange)	Butter, fats, oils, soft drinks, fruit juices, ice creams	Erythrosine	Maraschino cherries
Canthoxanthin (Orange red-red)	Soups, meat and fish dishes	Fast green FCF	Beverages, puddings, ice cream, sherbet, confections
Paprika (Orange-red)	Meat products, snack soups, salad	Indigo carmine	Confections, ice cream, dairy products
Saffron (Yellow)	Baked goods, rice dishes, meat dishes, soups	Sunset yellow FCF	Bakery products, ice cream, sauces, cereals, beverages
Leutin (Yellow)	Ice creams, dairy products, sugar, flour	Tartrazine	Beverages, cereals, bakery products, ice cream, sauces

Flavouring agents

The substances or additives added to food products, and which are responsible for change or enhancement in their taste, aroma or texture are called as flavouring agents or flavours. They are used in wide range of foods including baked goods, candies, soft drinks, and processed foods. They are known to enhance or modify the taste and aroma of food products, which is generally during food processing. They are available in various forms such as liquids, powders or extracts and should be added in least necessary quantity.

Applications of flavouring agents

The various applications of flavouring agents in food industry can be listed as below:

1. They enhance taste and aroma of food products. For example, vanilla extract is added to baked goods like cakes and cookies to give them a sweet, vanilla flavour.

2. They mask or cover up unpleasant smell of food products. For example, citrus flavours are often used in soft drinks to mask the bitter taste of caffeine.

3. They create unique flavour combinations which are not found in nature. For example, a strawberry cheesecake flavoured yogurt may use both natural and artificial flavouring agents to create a unique taste.

4. They standardize the flavour of a food product in such a way that it tastes the same every time when produced. This is particularly important for mass-produced foods.

5. They extend shelf life of food products by masking any off flavours that may develop over time.

Classification of flavouring agents

Flavouring agents can be classified into two types viz. natural or artificial flavouring agents.

1. Natural flavouring agents

Natural flavouring agents are extracted from natural resources such as plants, herbs, spices, animals or microbial fermentation. After extraction, they can be either used in their natural form or in processed form suitable for human consumption. For example, vanilla extract, cinnamon, ginger, citrous oils, peppermint etc.

Cinnamon sticks

Peppermint plant

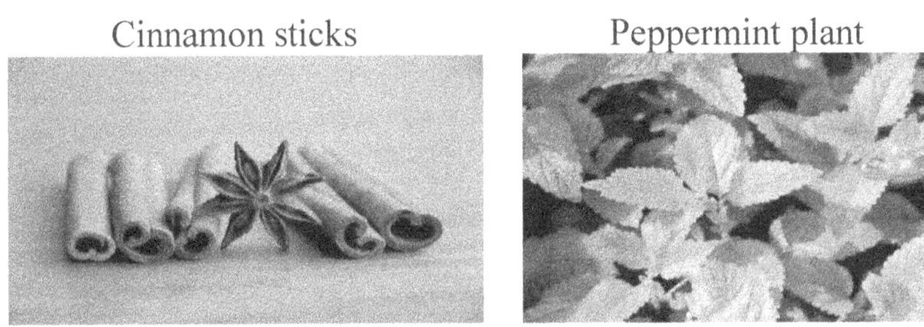

Ginger

Figure 3. Natural flavouring agents

2. Artificial flavouring agents

Artificial flavouring agents are synthesized in laboratories. They are chemically like natural flavouring agents but are easily available and less expensive.

They too face certain limitations. For example, sometimes artificial flavouring agents are not exact copy of natural flavouring agents, but they simply imitate them. For example, vanillin (vanilla flavour), amyl acetate (banana flavour) and ethyl butyrate (pineapple flavour).

Emulsifying agents

The process of dispersing one immiscible liquid into another immiscible liquid is called as emulsification. In simple words, emulsification means combining two or more liquids that usually cannot mix. Emulsification takes place in presence of some foreign substance. Such foreign substances which are responsible for emulsification process are called as emulsifying agents or emulsifiers. For example, oil and water are two immiscible liquids, they will mix only in presence of an emulsifier.

Emulsifiers are added to food products to create a smooth texture and to extend shelf life. They are normally hidden but maintain consistency and shape of food products. Also, they provide excellent palate for creativity and allow us to offer new flavour combinations. Common emulsifiers include egg yolk, mustard or honey and examples of food products including emulsifiers are low-fat spreads, margarine, salad dressings and many other creamy sauces.

Preservatives (संरक्षक)

Food preservation means keeping food products safe, suitable for human eating and avoiding food degradation. This is an important aspect of food industry. In ancient times, man has used salt (salting) and smoke (curing) to preserve meat and fish from degrading. Today life has become hasty, and people are more interested in packed food items, and this has increased the demand for food preservation techniques.

The substances or additives added to food products for preserving them for longer time or improving their taste are called as preservatives. Preservatives protect food products from deterioration causing microorganisms (bacteria, yeast and moulds) and food poisoning. Microorganisms generally breed easily on high-risk food products viz. meat, seafood, cheese and dairy products. Physical factors (viz. temperature and light) and chemical factors (viz. oxidation) can also spoil the food products. In addition, certain food products may turn rancid or change their colour in absence of preservatives. Thus, in all these situations, presence of preservatives is must for protecting food products and increasing their shelf life. Few processing methods including canning, dehydration (drying) smoking, salting, freezing and packaging can also be used as food preservation methods. For example, canning of jams and tomato sauce, preparation of dried fruits by drying fresh fruits, addition of salt etc.

Classification of food preservatives

Food preservatives can be classified into two classes based on sources from which they are extracted viz. preservatives obtained from natural sources and synthetically produced.

1. Preservatives obtained from natural sources

These can be obtained from natural sources such as plants, animals, and microorganisms such as bacteria, fungi and algae. For example, natamycin (E235), a widely used preservative in cheese and sausages can be obtained from soil bacteria. Salt and sugar are natural food preservatives used in pickles or sauerkraut.

2. Preservatives synthetically produced

These are synthesized in laboratory and used to prevent food contamination. For example, Nitrite, used in processed meats and poultry, helps to develop the characteristic colour and flavour and controls lipid oxidation, Butyrated hydroxyanisole (BHA), butyrated hydroxytoluene (BHT) and potassium sorbate.

The use of synthetic preservatives has few limitations. Synthetic preservatives being petroleum based can cause skin irritation in some individuals. Also, some time they need very narrow pH range to operate effectively.

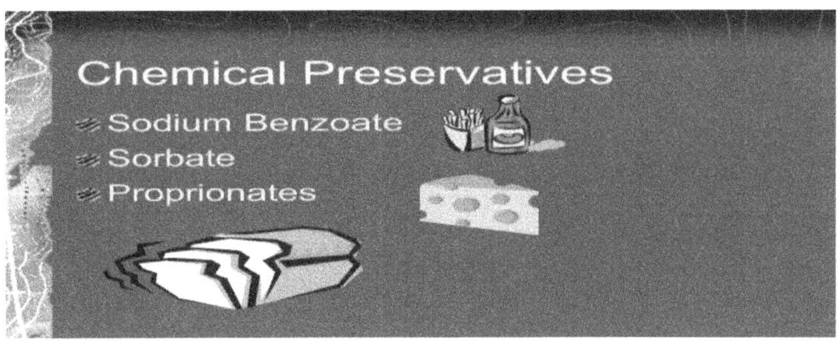

Preservatives good or bad?

These days we hear a hot discussion on whether the use of preservatives is good or bad? Few preservatives, for example sulphite group preservatives and benzoic acid and derivatives, cause breathing difficulties, shortness of breath, wheezing or coughing like symptoms in sensitive individuals. Apart from these, rest of the preservatives are generally regarded as safe for most consumers.

Leavening agents

Baked products, such as bread, cake or cookies, have increased volume due to trapped air which is achieved by food additives or substances added. These substances, which causes dough expansion by releasing gas when mixed with liquid, acid or heated during food processing, are called as leavening agents or rising agents. In simple words, leavening agents provide gas to the food products. These substances give baked products optimal volume, texture and crumb to make them swell and feel lighter which is pleasant to the mouth. Examples of leavening agents include baking soda or baking powder, whipped egg whites or cream, active or instant dry yeast, and even steam.

Taste enhancers

The word 'taste' in general to refer both smell and taste of food products. As such the term 'taste enhancers' would refer to substances that enhance or improve the sensation of food products in mouth. In simple words, the substances which improve or modify the aroma or taste of food products are called as taste enhancers. Human being is able to taste five tastes including sweet, sour, salty, bitter and umami (a Japanese word for 'pleasant savory taste' meaning 'meaty'). The substances such as monosodium L-glutamate (MSG), disodium 5'-inosinate (IMP), disodium 5'-(guanylate) (GMP), sodium chloride (NaCl) and sweeteners when added to food products can improve sensation of food in our mouth and are called as taste enhancers. Table 4 below represents taste enhancers used in food industry.

Table 4. Few important taste enhancers

Compound	Uses
Glutamic acid	Salt substitute in sausages, savory snacks, savory foods
Monosodium L-glutamate (MSG)	Canned vegetables, canned tuna, dressings, frozen foods
Disodium guanylate	Instant noodles, potato chips and snacks, savory rice, tinned vegetables, cured meats, packet soup
Disodium inosinate	Instant noodles, potato chips and snacks, savory rice, tinned vegetables, cured meats, packet soup
Maltol	Baked goods, chocolate substitute, soft and frizzy drinks, ice cream, jam

Antioxidants

Oxidation in human body creates free radicals which damage to cell membranes, cellular proteins, lipids and DNA in the body. The overload of free radicals can lead to certain conditions or diseases including vision loss, arthritis, Parkinson's or Alzheimer's disease, heart-liver diseases and various types of cancers along with ageing process.

Antioxidants are mostly found in fruits and vegetables as well as food including nuts, wholegrains, meat, poultry, fish etc. and can prevent this damage by scavenging and neutralising the free radicals. Examples include nutrient antioxidants, vitamins A, C and E, minerals such as copper, zinc and selenium and phytochemicals in plants (also called as non-nutrient antioxidants). Figure 4 represents chemical structures of few antioxidants.

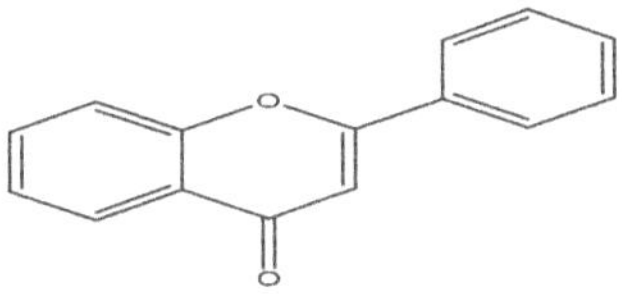

Flavonoids

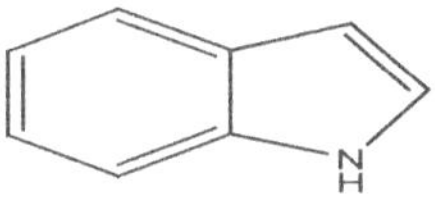

Indoles

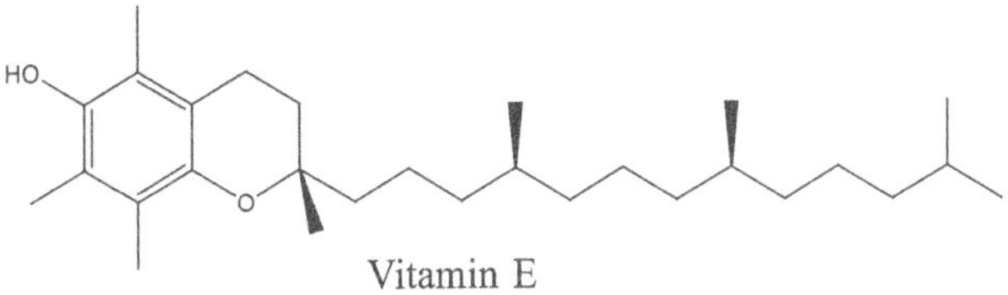

Vitamin E

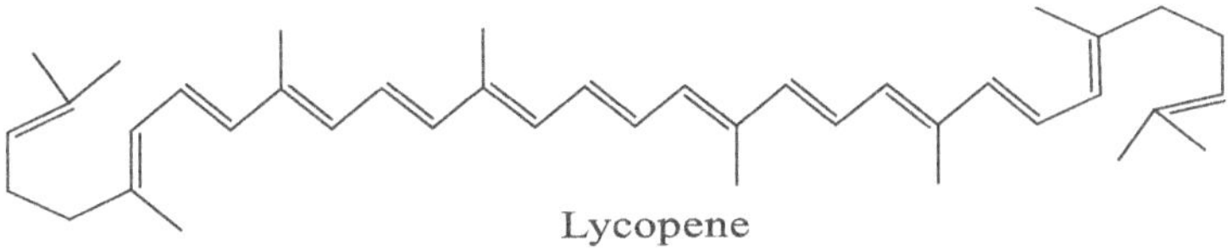

Lycopene

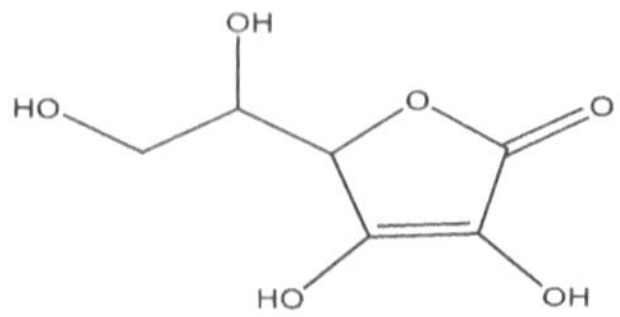

OH
HO
O
O
HO
OH
Vitamin C

Figure 4. Chemical structures of few antioxidants

Table 5 represents list of specific antioxidants and their sources.

Antioxidant	Sources
Allium sulphur compounds	Leeks, onions, garlic
anthocyanins	Eggplant, grapes, berries
Beta-carotene	Pumpkin, mangoes, apricots, carrots, spinach, parsley
catechins	Red wine and tea
Copper	Seafood, lean meat, milk and nuts
Cryptoxanthins	Red capsicum, pumpkin, mangoes
Flavonoids	Tea, green tea, citrus fruits, red wine, onion, and apples
Indoles	Cruciferous vegetables such as broccoli, cabbage and cauliflower
Isoflavonoids	Soybeans, tofu, lentils, peas and milk
Lignans	Sesame seeds, bran, whole grains and vegetables
Lutein	Green leafy vegetables like spinach and corn
Lycopene	Tomatoes, apricots, pink grapefruit and watermelon
manganese	Seafood, lean meat, milk and nuts
Polyphenols	Herbs
Selenium	Seafood, affal, lean, meat and whole grains
Vitamin A	Liver, sweet potatoes, carrots, milk and egg yolks
Vitamin C	Oranges, blackcurrants, kiwifruit, mangoes, broccoli, spinach, capsicum and strawberries
Vitamin E	Vegetable oils (Such as wheatgerm oil), avocados, nuts, seeds, and whole grains
Zinc	Seafood, lean meat, milk and nuts
Zoochemicals	Red meat, affal and fish. Also derived from the plants that animals eat.

Soft drinks, its ingredients and health effects.

Soft drinks are any class of non-alcoholic beverages which are usually carbonated or contain carbon dioxide (which is not compulsory though). They also contain natural or artificial sweetener, edible acids, natural or synthetic flavours, and sometimes juice.

Role of carbon dioxide in soft drinks

The carbon dioxide in soft drinks perform three functions:

1. It provides a cooling sensation, as gas is evaporated while drinking which helps extraction of heat from tongue.

2. It lowers the degree of acidity (pH 2.2-3.6) which slows down the growth of microorganisms.

3. It poisons the air present above soft drink, restricting the fungal growth due to lack of oxygen.

Ingredients in soft drinks

The various ingredients in soft drinks are listed below.

1. Water

Water is major component and occupy 82-97% part of a carbonated soft drink. The quality of water used can affect taste, appearance, physical and microbiological stability of soft drinks. The water to be used in soft drink preparation should be free from suspended matter and microorganisms i.e. it should have low bacterial count.

2. Sweetener

Sweetness is most important feature of a soft drink. Natural or synthetic sweeteners are used. **Natural sweeteners:** Glucose, Sucrose, Fructose, Maltose, Lactose, Steviol glycosides.

Synthetic sweeteners: Saccharine, Acesulfame-K. Cyclamate, Sucralose, Aspartame, Neotame, Alitame, Talin.

Recently, combination of more than one sweetener is used which is more economical. Examples include use of saccharin and cyclamate, aspartame, saccharin/aspartame mixtures in soft drinks industry. The aim is to imitate taste, stability and to create new taste. Figure 5 represents chemical structure of few sweeteners used.

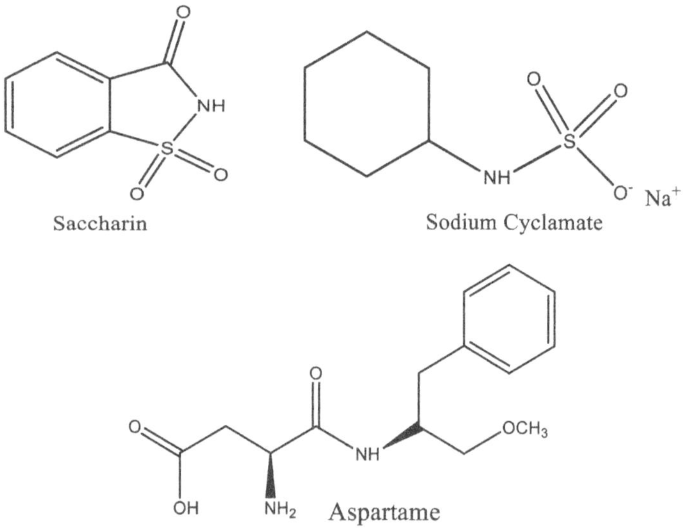

Figure 5. Chemical structures of few sweeteners

3. Acids

Acids present in soft drink modify sweetness of sugar and act as mild preservatives by reducing the pH level of the product. The common acids used are citric acid, tartaric acid, phosphoric acid, lactic acid, malic acid, fumaric acid, acetic acid and ascorbic acid.

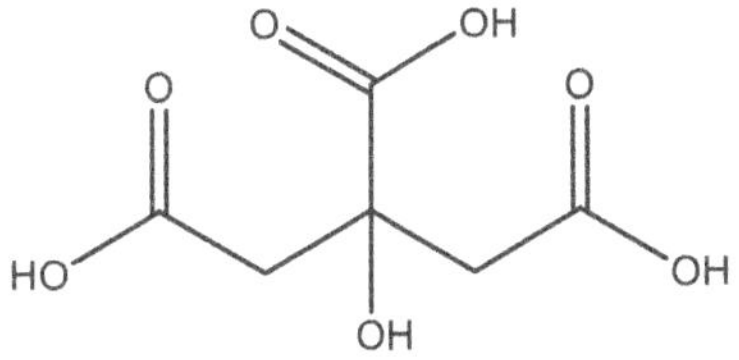

Citric acid

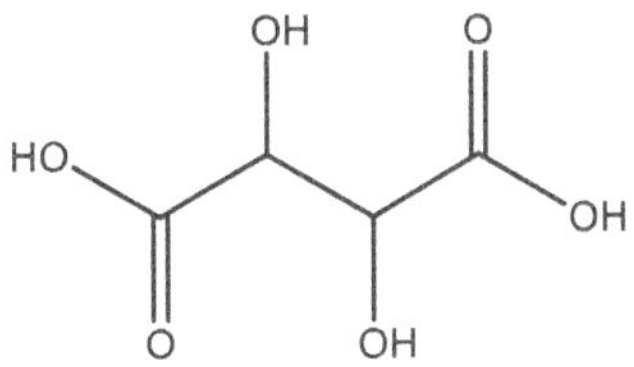

Tartaric acid

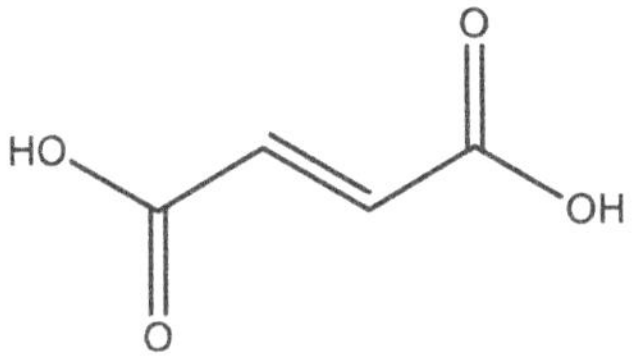

Fumaric acid

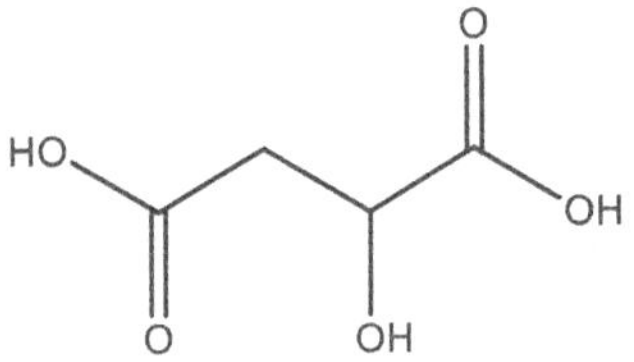

Malic acid

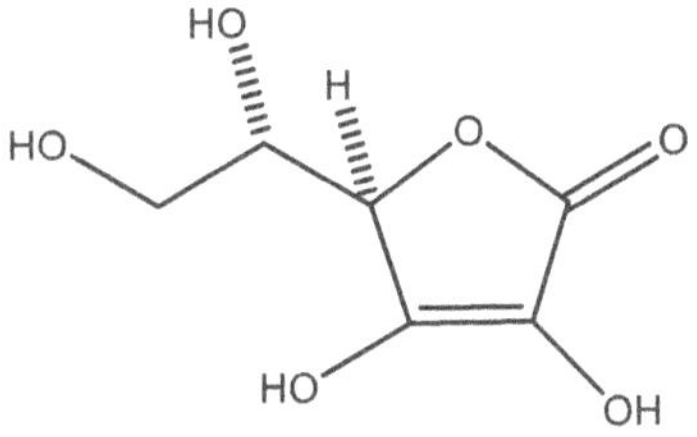

Ascorbic acid

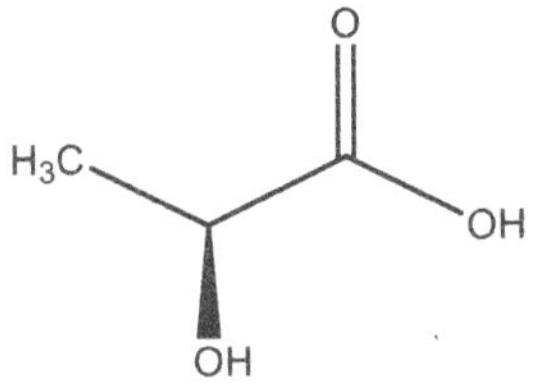

Lactic acid

Figure 6. Chemical structures of acids used in soft drinks

4. Colouring agents

Colouring agents improve the appearance of soft drinks and make them more presentable to the consumers. Natural or synthetic colouring agents are used.

Natural colouring agents: Anthocyanin, Beetroot red, Carmine, Annatto, β-Carotene, Paprika, Lutein, Curcumin, Chlorophylls.

Synthetic colouring agents: Quinine yellow, Tartrazine, Sunset yellow, Carmosine, Ponceau 4R, Patent blue FCF, Indigotin, Brilliant blue FCF.

5. Flavouring agents

Flavouring agents holds great significance and share 50% of total raw material cost in beverage formulation. The various flavouring agents used are Citrous flavours, orange flavours, Lime, Grapefruit, Cranberry, Cherry, Pomegranate, Pineapple flavours, Coconut and winter fruits. New flavours such as mango tango, apple splash, Fanta, raspberry and cranberry and Britvic 55 are also used.

6. Clouding agents

Clouding agents make soft drinks opalescent and look natural with low juice content. They can also mask sedimentation and ringing (where colouring/flavouring agents rise to surface of container). The various clouding agents used include pectin, gelatine, glyceryl acetate, brominated vegetable oils, sucrose acetate, dibenzoate and tribenzoate etc.

Health effects

Soft drinks, especially carbonated ones, can have several side effects on human health which can be listed as below:

1. Diabetes mellitus: Individuals, who, drinks soft drinks on regular basis are at more risk to develop type II diabetes mellitus.

2. Obesity: Soft drinks include sugar, which increase the calorie intake. As a result, regular consumption of soft drinks can lead to obesity.

3. Heart diseases: Studies have shown that individuals who consume soft drinks are regular basis are at a high risk of a heart attack. The heart diseases may be caused due to obesity, diabetes and high blood pressure associated.

4. Bone health: Regular consumption of soft drinks can damage bone health due to presence of high phosphate levels which may replace calcium levels in bone and make them brittle.

5. Tooth decay: Excess sugar and acid in fizzy drinks can cause dissolution of tooth enamel which can lead to dental caries or tooth decay, especially in children.

Food adulteration, food laws and standards.

Addition of contaminants into food items or beverages for the sake of increasing quality or decreasing price is called as food adulteration. In short, food adulteration is mixing of similar looking elements or compounds in food products to lower its quality and to increase the profit margin. Food adulteration can sometimes lead to serious illnesses including heart, kidney, liver and many other organ diseases in both humans and animals. Food adulteration, in overly populated country like India, is a major and serious issue.

Examples of food adulteration include, mixing of milk with water, mixing of pulses with sand particles, pebbles, mixing of oil with chemical derivatives or cheaper oils, packing low quality food products with high quality and fresh ones.

Food adulterants (अन्न भेसळ)

The substances or additives added to food products to degrade its quality or increase profit are called as food adulterants. They either lower the potency of the food products or reduce their nutritional value and are harmful. Some of them can lead to serious disease such as cancer and are hence lethal. Table 6 below listed food products and adulterants commonly added to them.

Table 6. Food products and adulterants

Article	Adulterant
Baking powder	Citric acid
Spices	Lead or lead chromate in Haldi, sawdust, sand
Starchy foods	Arrowroot powder, sand and dust
Coffee and tea	Chicory, husk, used tea dust, grit
Milk	Water, abstraction of fat
Vanaspati	Excessive hydrogenation, animal fat
Arhar Dal	Metanil yellow
Mustard seed	Argemone seeds
Non-alcoholic beverages	Saccharin, copper, lead and arsenic

Classification of food adulteration

Degradation of food quality by addition of some foreign substance is food adulteration. Food adulteration is further classified into two types viz. intentional and unintentional food adulteration.

1. Intentional food adulteration

When food adulterants are added into food products purposely or deliberately with an intention to increase the profit by manufacturer, supplier, retailer or any other person involved in food processing is called as intentional food adulteration. For example, when pebbles, stones, marbles, sand, mud, filth, chalk powder is mixed in food products, water is added in milk, or drinking water is contaminated etc. is food adulteration.

2.Unintentional or accidental food adulteration

When food adulteration occurs due to negligence while handling food products by the manufacturer, supplier, retailer or any other person involved in food processing then it is called as unintentional or accidental food adulteration. For example, presence of residues of peptides, droppings or rodents, larvae growth etc. in food products.

How to check food adulteration?

Checking food adulteration, in some cases, is possible using simple techniques. For example,

1. Adulteration in milk with detergents is checked by taking it in a bottle and adding water to it. After shaking if it forms a thick layer it is adulterated.

2. Adulteration in milk/sugar/jiggery using chalk powder is checked by mixing the sample in a glass of water. If any precipitate is formed at the bottom of glass, it indicates the presence of chalk.

3. Vegetables polished with colour can be checked by soaking them in water for some time. If the colour is dissolved, it can be observed in the water.

Food laws and standards

Food laws are formulated to prevent food adulteration and to ensure safe, healthy and good quality food products are provided to the consumers. The entire procedure of production, manufacturing, selling or distribution of food products is under observation of food laws.

The set of rules and regulations established by any Government to ensure food quality and safety is called as food safety standards. The aim is to reduce risk of contamination, chances of foodborne illnesses, and to protect workers in near contact to food products and consumers. All aspects of food production including collection of ingredients and materials, processing, packing and distribution are covered. Also, these standards aim for transparency, traceability and accountability of any organization related with food industry.

Sections 272 and 273 of Indian Penal Code (IPC), 1860 is related to the offence of food adulteration and drinks. There is a provision of six months' imprisonment or fine of INR 1000 to the person found guilty of food adulteration.

Various acts formulated in this regard are listed below:

1. The Calcutta Municipal Act, 1923

2. The Punjab Pure Food Act, 1929

3. The Bihar Prevention of Food Adulteration Act, 1948

4. The UP Pure Food Act, 1950

5. Fruit Products Order, 1955

6. Meat Food Products Order, 1973

7. Vegetable Oil Products (Control) Order, 1947

8. Edible Oils Packaging (Regulation) Order 1988

9. Solvent Extracted Oil, De-oiled Meal and Edible flour (Control) Order, 1967

10. Milk and Milk Products Order 1992

The acts formulated by various states in India before independence differ in methods of food analysis, punishments, implementation and standards. As such there was no uniformity and to overcome this issue, Indian Government, approved the Food Adulteration Committee (FAC) in 1943, which advised for central legislation to be formed in country and thus, the Prevention of Food Adulteration Act (PFA) came into force in 1954.

The Prevention of food adulteration (PFA) Act 1954

The act was passed in 1954 but came into effect on 15th June 1955 and extends to entire country. It includes total 25 sections. The act defines food adulteration and speaks about penalties that are levied on the vendor upon violation of the laws.

The act gives a variety of responsibilities to the central government and aims to prevent adulteration of food and beverage items, excluding water and drugs to make them fit for human consumption. Since 1955, the act has been amended three times in 1964, 1976 and 1986.

Essentials commodities act 1955

This act prevents retailers from illegally holding and selling essential commodities, thus restricting stockpiling or black marketing. The necessary items listed under the act include pulses and edible oils, pharmaceuticals, fertilizers, and petroleum and petroleum derivatives.

This act came into effect on 1st April 1955 by Indian Government and covers the entire country.

The act includes total 16 sections and a schedule.

Section 3, an important section of the act, speaks about power of central government to issue orders for controlling and prohibiting the production, supply and distribution of essential commodities. Section 7, another important section, speaks about penalties to the individuals who contravenes any order made under section 3.

The Food Safety and Standards Act 2006

The act came into effect on 23rd August 2006 and covers entire country. It includes 12 chapters, 101 sections and two schedules. Chapter 9 is an important chapter of this act which speaks about offences and penalties for crimes related to food safety. This act is important as it consolidated all the above listed acts.

The Food Safety and Standards Authority of India (FSSAI)

The FSSAI was established in 2008 under Ministry of Health and Family Welfare in India with an aim to regulate food processing so that safe, healthy and good quality food products can be provided for human consumption. All the related food processes including manufacture, storage, distribution, sale and import are covered under this act.

It is single reference point for handling all matters related to food quality and standards and is assisted by scientific committees and panels and central advisory committee which helps in setting standard and coordinate. The head office of is located in New Delhi, India.

*****

Question Bank

1. What are food colours? How are they classified?

2. What are flavoring agents? What are their applications?

3. Give classification of flavoring agents.

4. Define emulsifying agents? Give their applications.

5. What are food preservatives? How are they classified?

6. Define leavening agents. Give their classification.

7. Define taste enhancers. Which are common taste enhancers in daily use?

8. What are antioxidants? Give common examples.

9. What are soft drinks? Explain common ingredients in soft drinks.

10. Discuss adverse health effects of regular soft drinks use.

11. What is food adulteration? Give common examples of food adulteration.

12. How food adulteration is classified? How to check it?

13. Enlist the various acts formulated for prohibiting food adulteration.

14. Discuss 'PFA Act 1954'.

15. Discuss 'Essentials Commodities Act 1955'.

16. Discuss the 'Food Safety and Standards Act 2006'.

References

1. https://en.wikipedia.org

2. https://www.britannica.com

3. Food Colours and their Chemistry. Dr. Namita Gandhi. Journal of Agricultural Engineering and Food Technology. 6(2), April-June 2019, 129-132.

4. https://foodsafetyhelpline.com

5. https://foodinsight.org

6. https://byjus.com

7. https://www.gerdhelp.com

8. https://kitchenaid.com

9. https://epgp.inflibnet.ac.in

10. https://www.sciencedirect.com

11. https://www.healthline.com

12. https://ksyed.weebly.com

13. https://ssrana.in

14. https://www.indiacode.nic.in

15. https://www.fssai.gov.in

16. https://dfpd.gov.in

17. https://wbconsumers.gov.in

18. https://foodregulatory.fssai.gov.in

19. https://corpseed.com

CHAPTER- 3

Chemistry of plastics.

Introduction, Plastic in everyday life, plastic and polymers, classification of polymers, polymerisation reaction.

Application of plastics: Polyethylene, low density polyethylene, high density polyethylene, polypropylene, polyvinyl chloride, polyethylene terephthalate and acrylonitrile-butadiene-styrene. Environmental hazards and recycling of plastics

Introduction

Plastic is a high molecular weight polymer. It is prepared using various synthetic or semi-synthetic organic compounds. It is available in low cost, resistant to corrosion, is poor conductor of heat and electricity. In addition, it is lightweight in appearance, transparent, opaque and can be molded into variety of shapes as per need. These properties have made useful for variety of applications in human life. As such, since its discovery till today plastic has occupied every part of our life. We cannot imagine a day without plastic.

Although useful, plastic is non-biodegradable. That means, it is not degraded in the environment. Once prepared, it can remain on earth for many years. In addition, it can release chemicals which cause environmental pollution. As a result, the huge number of plastics used in daily applications has created a global concern and has become harmful to oceans, wildlife and human life also.

Plastic in everyday life

Plastic is everywhere in our life. We can't imagine our life without plastic. In fact, we use plastic in a variety of forms viz. polythene bags, bottles, toys, chairs, tables, boxes, suitcase, containers, trays, toothbrushes, pens, helmets, goggles, electrical wires, fire resistant fabrics, car parts etc. in daily applications.

1. Household items

Plastic is used in many household items such as bottles, mugs, buckets, toothbrush holders, pens, kitchen equipments, home electronics, flooring, curtains, paints etc.

2. Food and catering industry

Plastic is used in many packaging items useful for food and drinks which includes plastic bags, containers, disposable dishes and films. For example, PET bottles, polystyrene dishes, heat sealable polypropylene trays and polyethylene drinking straws.

3. In commerce

Plastic in used for commercial applications such as for making bags and packaging used for securing, carrying or shipping goods. In addition, billboards, stands, plaques, wall panels, signs and souvenirs (pen, key rings, scrapers etc.) are also made using plastics.

4. Fashion industry

Fashion industry is one of the fastest growing industries today. Plastics find wide range of applications in fashion industry. For example, the polymer called as polyester, a flexible, water-resistant synthetic fibre, is used for making blouses, sweaters, jackets, underwear and home textiles. Similarly, polyamide, an extremely lightweight, flexible and soft synthetic fibre is used for sportswear, swimwear, hosiery and tights.

5. Construction industry

Plastic is also useful in construction industry. For example, insulation and protection materials (including films, foams, sealing tapes), fitting and finishing materials (cladding, floor panels, PVC carpets, composite terrace boards), water supply and sewage pipes, protective pipes etc. used in construction industry are made of plastics.

Plastic and polymers

The term polymer in Greek means 'many parts. A polymer is basically obtained by combining many small molecules or substances, called as monomers, using variety of combinations. In short, polymers are long chain macromolecules. Polymers are present all around us. Natural polymers are found in plants and animals. The cellulose, starch, silk, wool, proteins, nucleic acids (DNA & RNA) found in plants and animals are examples of natural polymers.

Polymers can also be made in laboratories. Such polymers are called as synthetic polymers. Plastics are high molecular weight polymers which are made from synthetic or semi-synthetic organic compounds. Thus, plastics are man-made polymers. Common examples of plastics include polyethylene terephthalate (PET), low- and high-density polyethylene (LDPE and HDPE), polyvinyl chlorides (PVC), polypropylene (PP) and polystyrene (PS) etc.

Classification of polymers

Polymers are complex molecules and hence cannot be classified in unique way. The simple classification includes differentiating them based on source of availability. As such polymers can be classified into three types as follows:

1. Natural polymers

These are found in plants and animals. These are generally formed by addition or condensation polymerisation processes. Examples include nucleic acids (DNA and RNA), proteins, starch, cellulose and rubber. The polymers which are degradable in the environment are called as biopolymers. These are also included under the name natural polymers.

2. Semi-synthetic polymers

These are obtained from natural polymers and undergo further chemical modifications as per requirement. The modifications are useful to enhance their quality. Examples include Rayon, vulcanized rubber, gun cotton, cellulose nitrate, cellulose acetate.

3. Synthetic polymers

The man-made polymers are called as synthetic polymers. These are synthesised in chemical laboratories using variety of chemicals and reactions. They are applicable in industries and various dairy products. Examples include nylon-66, polyethylene, polyester, Teflon and epoxy.

Alternate classification of polymers

Alternatively, polymers can be classified as thermosets, thermoplastics, fibres and elastomers.

1. Thermosets

The plastics which are permanently hardened through curing process are called as thermosets. The curing process involves applications of various processes such as heating, passing radiation, applying high pressure or catalyst to the pre-polymer liquid or soft solid to make it hard. These consist of a cross-linked structure of heavily branched molecules. Common examples include epoxy, silicone, polyurethane, and phenolic. Thermosets or thermosetting polymers find wide range of applications in food packaging, bumpers, credit cards preparations etc.

2. Thermoplastics

These are plastics which can be softened and melted by heating but set again when cooled. This can be repeated many times without changing materials' chemical or molecular structure which means thermoplastics are recyclable. Thermoplastics are lightweight, durable and resistant to chemicals. Common examples include polyethylene, polypropylene, polyvinyl chloride, polystyrene, polycarbonate, polyethylene terephthalate etc. The thermoplastics find wide range of applications including packaging, automotive parts, medical devices and consumer goods etc.

3. Elastomers

These are rubber like materials and have viscosity and elasticity. They deform under pressure and return to their original shape when is pressure is released. These are polymers with weak intermolecular forces, high failure strain and low Young's modulus. Examples include natural rubber, polyurethanes, polybutadiene, silicone and neoprene etc. Elastomers find wide range of applications in motor vehicles (tyres, seals), consumer products (shoe soles to baby pacifiers), construction materials (adhesives and sealants), industrial products (belts, molds, lubricants), wire and cables and medical products etc.

4. Plastic fibres

These are obtained using spinning process. In this a polymeric liquid is extruded through fine holes called spinnerets, thus resulting into fibres of specific lengths. The process increases crystallinity and strength of fibres. These are linear, branched or cross-linking (network) polymers. Common examples include polyethylene terephthalate (PET), polyethylene (PE), polyoxymethylene (POM), polypropylene (PP) and polyvinyl alcohol (PVA).

Plastic fibres find wide range of applications in manufacture of paper, cigarette filters, hosiery, sports garments, seat belts, ropes, nets, fishing lines, aircraft panels, bulletproof vests, flame resistant clothing, blankets, sweaters, swimsuits etc.

Polymerisation reaction

Polymerisation is a chemical reaction in which a large number of small molecules i.e. monomers are combined to produce a macromolecule with high molecular mass i.e. polymer. The polymer obtained may have a linear or branched chain structure. In short, polymerisation is a polymer formation process.

It generally includes three steps viz. initiation, propagation and termination. During initiation, the monomer acquires an active site and become a free radical. This starts the polymer formation reaction. Apart from free radicals, other initiators such as absorption of heat, light or irradiation can also initiate the reaction. In propagation step, the active monomers (which initiated the reaction) adds on to other monomers and the chain grows on increasing. The addition of active monomer on other monomers is a rapid process. In last and termination step, the polymer chain free radical reacts with other free radical, and the reactions stops.

Types of polymerisation reactions

Generally, polymerization reactions are of two types of viz. addition and condensation polymerization.

1. Addition polymerization

In this polymerization, monomers, with double or triple bonds, combine to form polymers without releasing by products. These reactions are generally carried out in presence of catalysts. The common catalysts used include titanium tetrachloride ($TiCl_4$), Ziegler-Natta catalyst (a mixture of titanium tetrachloride and triethyl aluminium) and Philips catalyst [Chromium (VI) oxide deposited on silica]. This polymerization follows chain-growth mechanism.

Polymers such as polyethylene, polypropylene, polyvinyl chloride etc. are prepared using addition polymerization.

H H
C===C   TiCl4 catalyst   H—C—C—C—H
H H
Ethylene   Polyethylene

Figure. Formation of polyethylene (Addition polymerization)

2. Condensation polymerization

In this polymerization, monomers combine to form polymers, while releasing small by-products such as water and methanol molecules during each addition of monomer unit. This polymerization follows a step-growth mechanism.

The monomers should have one or two functional groups. When both functional groups are difunctional a linear polymer resulted, while if one of the functional groups is tri- or tetra-functional, a cross-linked polymer is obtained. Common examples are alcohol, amine and carboxylic acid groups. Nylon 66 polymer is obtained by reacting adipic acid and hexamethylene diamine.

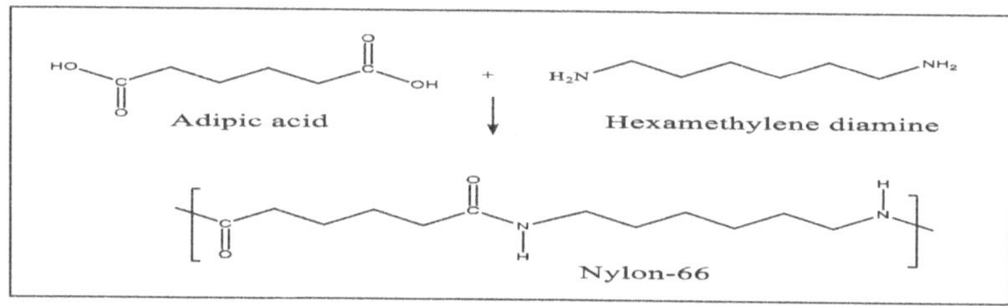

Figure. Formation of Nylon-66 polymer (Condensation polymerization)

Application of plastics

1. Polyethylene terephthalate (PET)

PET is used in mineral water, fizzy drink and beer bottles, pre-prepared food trays and roasting bags, as fibre for clothing and carpets and in some shampoo and mouthwash bottles.

2. Polyethylene (PE)

Polyethylene, also called as polythene, is a light, versatile synthetic resin obtained from combining ethylene monomer units. Ethylene ($CH_2=CH_2$) consists of two methylene (CH_2) units bonded with double bond which are broken using catalyst and resultant single bond is used to link with carbon atom of another ethylene molecule leading to polymer formation.

A variety of polyethylenes including high density polyethylene (HDPE), low density polyethylene (LDPE) and liner low density polyethylene (LLDPE) are available. Polyethylenes find a wide range of applications.

HDPE is used in detergent, bleach and fabric conditioner bottles, snack food boxes and cereal box liners, milk and non-carbonated drink bottles, toys, buckets, rigid pipes, crates, plant pots, plastic wood, garden furniture, wheeled refuse bins and compost containers. LDPE find applications in preparations of films, fertiliser bags, refuse sacks, packaging films, bubble wrap, flexible bottles, irrigation pipes, thick shopping bags for clothes and products, wire and cable applications and in some bottle tops.

3. Polyvinyl Chloride (PVC)

PVC is used in preparing credit cards, carpet backing and other floor covering, window and door frames, guttering pipes and fittings, power cables, telephone cables, data cables, wire and cable sheathing and synthetic leather products. It has been a significant raw material for manufacturing goods in building industry. It is the ideal material for surgical, pharmaceutical and medical applications.

4. Polypropylene (PP)

PP find applications in preparing most bottle tops, ketchup and syrup bottles, yoghurt and some margarine containers, potato crisp bags, biscuit wrappers, crates, plant pots, drinking straws, hinged lunch boxes, refrigerated containers, fabric or carpet fibres, heavy duty bags etc. it is used in automotive industries in car dashboards, bumpers, film padding, interior components, cladding, film skins etc.

5. Polystyrene (PS)

PS is applicable in preparing yoghurt containers, egg boxes, fast food trays, video cases, vending cups and disposable cut, seed trays, coat hangers, and low-cost brittle toys.

6. Acrylonitrile-butadiene-styrene (ABS)

ABS is a common thermoplastic polymer made by combining three monomers acrylonitrile, butadiene and styrene. Each of these three monomers contribute different property to the polymer. ABS finds wide range of applications in making pipe fittings, automotive body parts, wheel covers, electronics, computer keyboard keys, enclosures and protective head gears.

Environmental hazards due to plastics

Since the discovery of plastic, its use has been increased tremendously. Plastic is available at low cost and is convenient to use, thus it has occupied every part of our life. People are using million tonnes of plastic on daily basis around the world. But the progress has not come alone, there are few serious issues related with plastic use.

1. Chemicals released from plastic are added to soil and soil fertility is highly affected.

2. Waste plastics can cause blockage in the drains which leads to stagnant water. Such stagnant water can give rise to harmful diseases such as malaria, cholera etc.

3. Plastic takes decades to degrade in the environment. That means, once prepared, it will remain in the environment for a long time. This cause environmental pollution.

4. Burning of plastic release toxic gases into the environment which is dangerous to human health and the environment.

5. The plastic pollution interferes with nature and natural processes are affected, reducing ecosystems' ability to adapt climate change. This is harmful to human life.

6. The plastic production processes use petroleum on a large scale, which can deplete the available petroleum reservoir.

Recycling of plastics

Plastic recycling means collecting and processing plastic waste into some other useful products. The plastic waste from our home, offices and other places are collected and send to Material Recovery Facility (MRF) centres. The MRF centres sort these plastics waste according to types using various equipment and send for reprocessing. The selected plastic wastes are melted and extruded into a new recycled plastic pellets which are sold for use in new products. Thus, recycling can help in reduction of plastic pollution and protect the environment.

In 1988, the Society of the Plastics Industry (SPI) introduced the Resin Identification Code (RIC) system which divided all the plastics into seven different categories. The classification is based on the ability of plastic material to get recycled, ease of recycling and financial worth of the process. Based on this RIC system, few plastic types can be recycled.

1. Polyethylene terephthalate (PET)

PET is most widely recycled plastic in the world. The substantial parts of PET plastic are usually recycled into fashion items such as polar fleece clothes, backpacks and carpets. The innovative use of PET is as a construction material in third-world countries. In this application, plastic bottles are filled with sand, then stacked and either mudded or cemented together to form a wall.

2. High density polyethylene (HDPE)

HDPE is one of the easiest plastic polymers to recycle. It is converted into bottles for detergent, motor oil, household cleaners etc. and film packaging. It is also used in lower-value products such as plastic lumber, tables, roadside curbs, benches and other durable plastic products.

3. Polyvinyl chloride (PVC)

It is most hazardous plastic. The chemicals released include bisphenol A (BPA), phthalates, lead, dioxins, mercury and cadmium.

Many of these chemicals are carcinogens and cause allergic symptoms. Hence PVC is **not** recycled.

4. Low density polyethylene (LDPE)

LDPE is very cheap and low-quality plastic, and its recycling is not financially worthwhile. When recycled it can be transformed into bin liners and packaging films.

5. Polypropylene

Recycling polypropylene is difficult and expensive and hence not financially worth. In addition, recycled polypropylene is black or grey coloured which limits its applications. After recycled, it is mostly used in plastic lumbers, park benches, auto parts, speed bumps and for other industrial applications.

6. Polystyrene

When exposed to hot and oily food, the polystyrene products can release styrene which is toxic to brain and nervous system. It can also affect to genes, lungs, liver and the immune system. Hence it is **not** recycled.

7. Other plastic materials

All other plastic types not included in types 1-6 are included in this category. Polycarbonate (PC) is most common example of this type. PC is used for baby bottles, sippy cups, water bottles, water gallons, metal food can liners, ketchup containers and dental sealants.

PC release BPA, a chemical responsible for many health issues including chromosome damage in female ovaries, decreased sperm production in males, early onset of puberty and behavioural changes. It is also responsible for altered immune function, impaired brain and neurological functions, cardiovascular system damage, type 2 diabetes, obesity, various cancer risks and metabolic disorders. Hence it is **not** recycled.

****

Quaestion Bank

1. What is plastic? Explain its applications in daily life.

2. What is mean by polymer? Give classification of polymers.

3. What is polymerisation?

4. Discuss mechanisms involved in polymerization reaction.

5. Discuss types of polymerization reactions with suitable example.

6. Discuss various applications of polyethylene (PE).

7. Give various applications of polyvinyl chloride (PVC).

8. Give various applications of polypropylene (PP).

9. Discuss various environemntal hazards caused due to plastic use.

10. What is recycling of plastics? Which types of plastics can be recycled?

References

1. https://en.wikipedia.org

2. https://products.pcc.eu/

3. https://richfieldplastics.com

4. https://vedantu.com

5. https://testbook.com

6. https://www.bpf.co.uk

7. https://waste4change.com

8. https://www.plasticsforchange.org

CHAPTER- 4

Drugs chemistry.

Introduction

Classification of drugs.

Analgesics, antipyretics, antihistamines, antacids, tranquilizers, sedatives, antibiotics, antifertility drugs. (Name, structure, simple one preparation and uses are expected)

Introduction:

The word drug derived from French word "Drogue" which means a dry herb. Most of the disease is caused by microorganisms. Drugs which is single or combination of two or more compounds.

Drug is defined as "a chemical substance used in the diagnosis, prevention, treatment or cure the disease in human or animal being."

Or

A drug is a chemical substance that, when administered to a living organism, produces a biological effect.

According to World Health Organization (WHO), who promote basic health globally, "A drug is any substance or product that is used or intended to be used to modify or explore physiological system or pathological state for the benefit of the recipient". It is systematically defined as – "The use of drug (chemical compounds) to destroy infectious microorganism or inhibit their growth without damaging host cells or tissue of human body or animals".

Classification of drugs: -

Drugs are classified based on their therapeutic actions into two main classes, Functional drugs or pharmacodynamics agent and Chemotherapeutic agents.

1) Functional drugs: Functional drugs are also called as Pharmacodynamics agent. These types of drugs stimulate or depress the various function of the body without destroying the disease. They do not attack on pathogenic microorganism. Functional drugs are mainly used for non-infectious diseases to cure abnormal functions of the body. These are also classified into following types.

a) Analgesics (वेदनाशामक)

b) Antipyretics (त)

c) Antihistamines (पेशीजालात हिस्टॅमिनच्या स्वीकारास अडथळा आणणाऱ्या औषधांच्या गटातील कोणतेही एक औषध)

d) Antacids (आम्लता नष्ट करणारा अल्कलाइन पदार्थ)

e) Anaesthetics (वेदना जाणवणे बंद करणारा पदार्थ)

f) Anti-inflammatory (विरोधी दाहक)

g) Tranquillizers (चिंता कमी करणारे औषध)

h) Sedatives (उपशामक (औषध)

2) Chemotherapeutic agents:

These drugs used to treat & cure specific type of disease. These drugs are called chemotherapeutic agents. These drugs usually work by destroying invading organism without destroying the cells of infected host.

The various chemotherapeutic agents are as follows

a) Antimalarials (मलेरियाविरोधी)

b) Antibacterial (बॅक्टेरियाच्या वाढीस प्रतिबंध करणारा पदार्थ)

c) Antifungal (बुरशीविरोधी)

d) Antitubercular

e) Antibiotics (प्रतिजैविक)

f) Antiseptics (जंतुनाशक)

1. Name, structure, simple one preparation and uses of analgesic drug

Analgesics are drugs used for controlling pain. Drug that relieves pain without significantly impairing consciousness are called as analgesics.

e.g. Ibuprofen, Aspirin

Structure of Ibuprofen

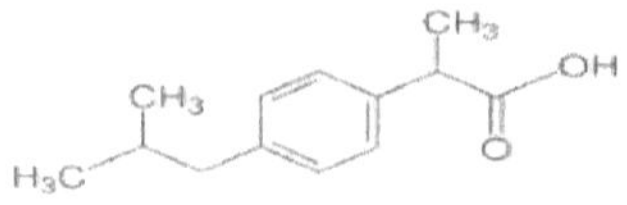

Synthesis of Ibuprofen

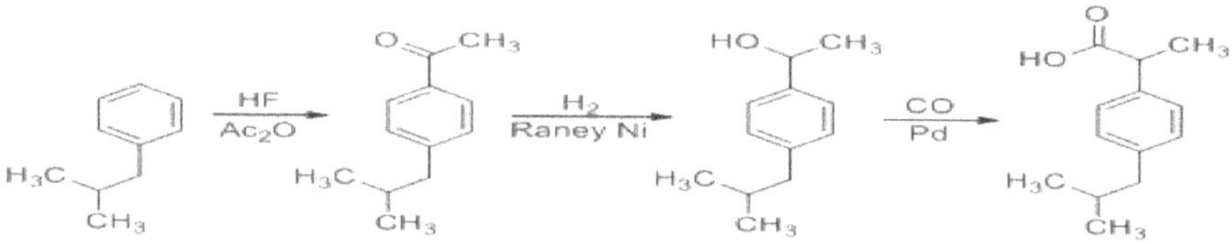

Scheme 1. BHC Company synthesis of ibuprofen

Uses

Ibuprofen is used to reduce fever and to relieve minor aches and pain from headaches, muscle aches, arthritis, menstrual periods, the common cold, toothaches, and backaches

2. Name, structure, simple one preparation and uses of antipyretic drug

Antipyretics are drugs that reduce fever. Antipyretics cause the hypothalamus to override an interleukin-induced increase in temperature. CNS especially hypothalamus maintain body temperature therefore it is called as body thermostat. The body will then work to lower the temperature, and the result is a reduction in fever. e.g. Paracetamol

Structure of Paracetamol (N-Acetyl-p-Aminophenol):

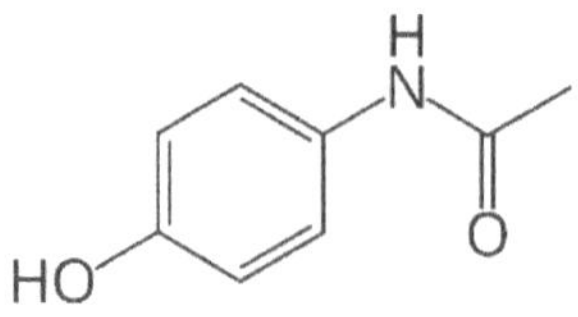

Synthesis of Paracetamol

It is prepared from p-Nitro phenol as follows.

Uses:

Paracetamol is classified as antipyretic and mild analgesic

3. Name, structure, simple one preparation and uses of antihistamines drug

Antihistamines are medications used to relieve allergy symptoms by blocking the effects of histamine. They come in various forms, including pills, chewable tablets, capsules, liquids, nasal sprays, and eye drops. Some examples of common antihistamines include cetirizine (Zyrtec), fexofenadine (Allegra), and levocetirizine (Xyzal)

Structure of Cetirizine

Synthesis of Cetirizine

Uses

Cetirizine is a second-generation antihistamine used to relieve symptoms of allergies, such as hay fever, allergic rhinitis, and urticaria. It works by blocking a chemical called histamine

4. Name, structure, simple one preparation and uses of antacids drug

An antacid is a substance which neutralizes stomach acidity and is used to relieve heartburn, indigestion, or an upset stomach. Some common examples include calcium carbonate (like Tums), magnesium hydroxide (like Milk of Magnesia), aluminium hydroxide (like Maalox), and combinations of these with simethicone to reduce gas

e.g. Omeprazole

Structure of Omeprazole

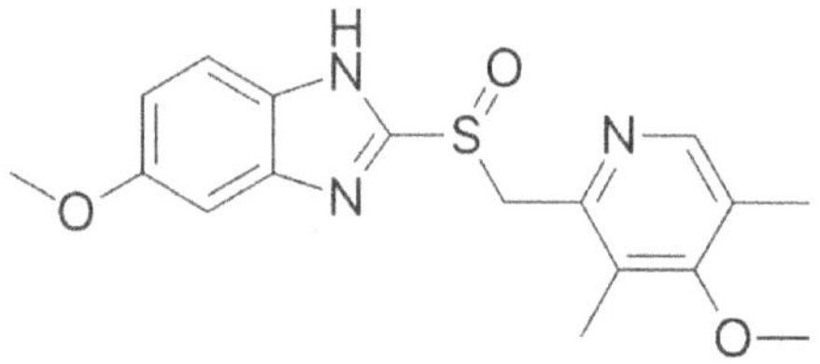

Synthesis of Omeprazole

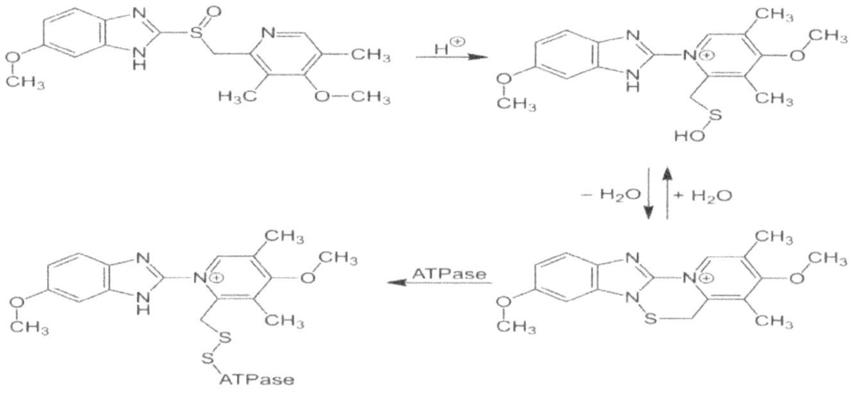

Uses

It is used to treat certain conditions where there is too much acid in the stomach. It is used to treat gastric and duodenal ulcers, erosive esophagitis, and gastroesophageal reflux disease (GERD).

5. Name, structure, simple one preparation and uses of tranquilizers,

Tranquillizers are drug that is used to reduce anxiety, fear, tension, agitation, and related states of mental disturbance. e.g. Diazepam

Structure of Diazepam

Synthesis of Diazepam

Uses

Diazepam is mainly used to treat anxiety, insomnia, panic attacks, and symptoms of acute alcohol withdrawal. It is also used as a premedication for inducing sedation, anxiolysis, or amnesia before certain medical procedures.

6. Name, structure, simple one preparation and uses of antibiotics

Antibiotics are the Substances or drugs that destroys or inhibits the growth of other microorganisms and is used in the treatment of external or internal infections. While some antibiotics are produced by microorganisms, most are now manufactured synthetically. The well-known example is penicillin and streptomycin. e.g. Amoxicillin

Structure of Amoxicillin

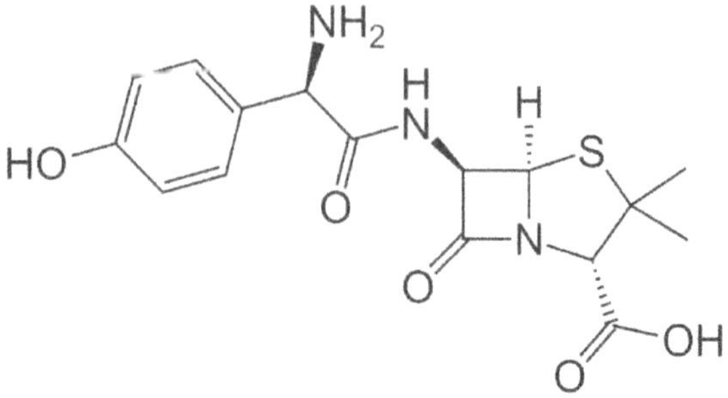

Synthesis of Amoxicillin

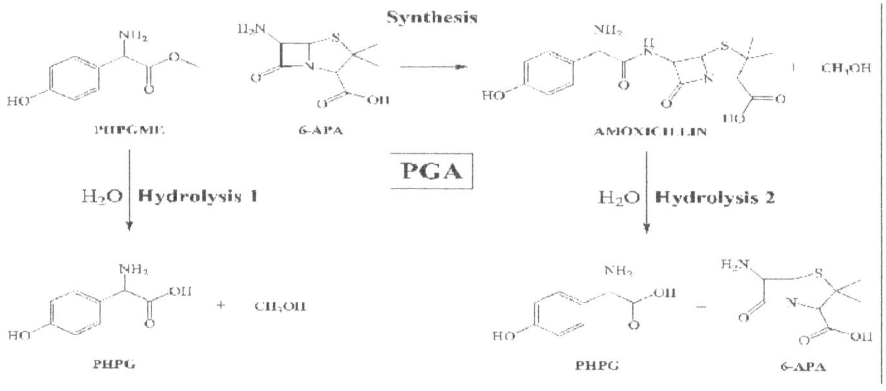

Uses

Amoxicillin is used to treat bacterial infections in many different parts of the body (ear, lungs, nose, sinus, skin, urinary tract). It is also used with other medicines (e.g., clarithromycin, lansoprazole) to treat H. pylori infection and duodenal ulcers.

Sedatives

An agent or a drug that produces a soothing, calming, or tranquilizing effect reducing or relieving anxiety, stress, irritability, or excitement.

Common examples include benzodiazepines like alprazolam (Xanax), lorazepam (Ativan)

Antifertility drugs

Antifertility drugs, also known as birth control pills or oral contraceptives, are medications used to prevent pregnancy by suppressing the hormones that control fertility.

Quaestion Bank

1. What is Drug ? Give characteristics of good drug.

2. Give the classification of Drugs.

3. What is antipyretic drug? Give structure, synthesis and uses of Paracetamol.

4. What is analgesic drug? Give structure, synthesis and uses of Ibuprofen.

5. What is antihistamine drug? Give structure, synthesis and uses of Cetirizine.

6. What is antacid drug? Give structure, synthesis and uses of Omeprazole.